THE MODERN

QUEER TAROT

A Seventy-Eight Card Deck &

LGBT History Primer

Written by Robert Barber & John Callaghan

Designed by Robert Barber & Tanya Wischerath

Illustrations by Tanya Wischerath

ISBN: 979-8-218-46677-0 (Hard Back)

979-8-218-46678-7 (Paper Back)

ACKNOWLEDGEMENTS

From Robert: Eternally grateful to my mother, Ellen Barber, and her friends Linda Flanagan and Leanne Lindsey, all of whom encouraged me when I was twelve years old to embrace and pursue my passion for astrology and Tarot.

From Robert & John: Monique Jenkinson – A big squeeze and huge thank you not just for your early and sustained enthusiasm for the deck, but also for your incredible and thorough work as a reader and editor on the text. We used all of your notes!

From Tanya: My special thanks to Kelly Hansen for feeding me cake and encouragement throughout the illustration process, Rachel Pollack for her wonderful insights on the Tarot, and Zoe Bott for all the woo.

ABOUT THE CREATORS

Robert Barber was raised in Las Vegas, NV, but has lived in San Francisco since 1997. He worked as a clerk and a reader at the Psychic Eye Book Shops in Las Vegas and San Francisco, and currently works at Crystal Way in the Castro District. He has dedicated much of the last thirty-five years to studying Western esotericism, in particular astrology, the Tarot and Kabbalah. Robert lives in the Haight-Ashbury with his husband John Callaghan and their cat in black, Cash.

John Callaghan is a native of Dublin, Ireland and holds an M.A. in Philosophy, Cosmology, and Consciousness from the California Institute of Integral Studies in San Francisco. A lifelong student of esoterica and metaphysics, he has a particular interest in the teachings of Carl Jung. Devoted cat owner and married to Robert Barber.

Tanya Wischerath, born in 1984, is a painter, illustrator and printmaker. Her work is a glorification of gender fluidity, performative sexuality, and the creation and sustainability of fantastic realities outside of heteronormativity. She lives in San Francisco with her partner/muse Kelly and their Grayhound Indigo

INTRODUCTION TO THE MODERN QUEER TAROT

The Modern Queer Tarot has been created as both a divinatory device, as with any tarot or contemporary oracle deck, and as a means to educate and/or remind readers of the lives of seventy-eight richly memorable LGBT persons from history; every card in the deck, both Major Arcana and Minor Arcana, is assigned to one of these queer persons.

The lives of these people are not meant to be reduced to the quality or qualities of the card they've been chosen to represent per se, but there is no doubt that each was appointed due to a large facet of their lives being typified by said qualities. By no means either does the deck say that these are the seventy-eight greatest queer people throughout history. Rather The Modern Queer Tarot was designed to find a balance between the people that best fit the interpretations of each card without sacrificing any of the inherent, long-honored divinatory meanings of the cards themselves.

Some people represented in the deck are particularly well-known, and little new information can be presented about them; however, their lives so perfectly fit the card that there was clearly no other choice, and the joy of associating them with it too ecstatic and gleeful for us to pass up. Many other people in the deck are quite unknown in comparison and it is with great pleasure that the opportunity to make them more eminent has arisen. The list of those people who didn't make it into the final cut of the deck is long, full of some regret and a few sighs, but in the end, they simply weren't the best choice for any of the cards.

The starting point in history from which we selected people for the deck was definitive. We began with German lawyer and writer, Karl Heinrich Ulrichs (1825-1895), our Ace of Swords. By 'begin,' we meant to only choose people born after he was, and more importantly, after his life's work was beginning to trickle down and dilute into modern society, albeit with much widespread opposition for many years. Ulrichs is credited with being the first person to define themselves as a homosexual (or an *urning* in his native German, *uranian* in English translation) because of identity and not behavior. He believed that non-heterosexual romantic love was natural and biological, and he spoke out in public in defense of it until his dying day, travelling all over the various Confederations of Germany and the Kingdom of Italy at the time, writing near twenty pamphlets, constantly risking not only incarceration, but physical harm as well. Ulrichs was without question the first person to out themselves in public, and to this day, the International Lesbian and Gay Law Association gives out a Karl Heinrich Ulrichs Award for the promotion of sexual equality.

Of course, later popularized and expanded on by many others, Ulrichs' pioneering beliefs cannot be overstated. Prior to him, no one ever publicly declared themselves to be a homosexual, queer, bisexual, lesbian, or transexual as an objective identity; rather, they may or may not have participated in *behavior* that could be labelled 'sodomy' or 'sapphic' out of sheer ignorance, spite and/or prejudice, but there was no queer community, there was no group that they could consider themselves apart of. Ulrichs took the first step in changing all of this and lit the spark for what we know today as the modern queer world.

For the first fifty years of the queer rights movement (1865-1915), the vast majority of those who could come out of the closet were almost always white, also rich and/or from the upper classes. Their money and social rank provided them with the means to live their lives as they wanted, free from financial reasons of needing to marry. Just the notion alone that people didn't need to marry was revolutionary at the time, for they found themselves earning enough on their own without an income from a spouse. No children meant even more money to keep, and more money meant more freedom. And, quite significantly, western economies began to favor city life. The middle-class was created and evolved. These unmarried, middle-class, or richer, people even began to live their sexual lives as they truly wanted, albeit still in clandestine ways, and very often in fear of getting caught, breaking the then strict sodomy laws.

Molly Houses, and their ilk, were not too uncommon in 18th and 19th century Britain, Scandinavia as well as continental Europe. These were places for queers to gather and meet sexual partners, just as much brothels as they were taverns or cafes. Raids were frequent, and punishments were harsh, so the movement to identify, organize, and politicize their sexuality was not at the forefront of their lives as queers at the time. Again, it took someone like Ulrichs, who was very often punished for his publicly spoken words and publications, to plant the seed of the nascent modern queers as we know them today.

In those early decades, many other men and women of means, now long-forgotten, made their sexuality known publicly. Though not always concerned with the notion of a queer rights movement itself, or for that matter even in choosing to run with like kind, all of them should be honored for publicly owning who they were (and also were not) and through their fortitude, independence and sacrifice leaving the world that much more tolerant of queers than when they were first born into it, for it is only by being seen that queers could (and can) come to be accepted.

With there being seventy-eight cards in a tarot deck, as well as limiting ourselves to only people who have died, we knew the deck was going to be laden with gay white men, as most of the folks doing the momentous work involving visibility for queer people of color and within the modern trans movements of today are, thankfully, still alive. However, we were committed to having as much visibility as possible within the deck for lesbians, bisexuals, queers of color and trans people, hence our dedication to half the deck (thirty-nine cards) being attributed to at least one of the aforementioned queer peoples. Also, it should be noted that four cards aren't individuals at all, but rather two are momentous direct action events, one is an influential theatre troupe, and another represents an international political organization; they were simply the best fit for the cards they correspond to, and perhaps even more so, too significant of events/people to not include in our attempt in giving the deck a truly comprehensive cover of queer history.

Unlike many tarot and oracle decks in the market today, we wanted the Modern Queer Tarot to cut no corners nor sugar-coat certain cards that, to us, are objectively, dispassionately, negative in their meaning. This required choosing queer people from history that are in no way role models. In fact, a few are malicious, malignant, and unquestionably vile, but their influence on, or participation in, the queer world is nevertheless undeniable.

Ultimately, we wanted the Modern Queer Tarot deck to be a microcosm for not only ourselves as writers, artists, tarot card readers and practitioners, but also for queer history itself, full of much color and vibrancy, darkness and shadows, humor and life, profound pain and abundant joy. We want the deck to be as much a helpful divinatory tool, granting insight towards the answers sought, assisting the querent however it can, as well as a fascinating picture book, a festive monograph of queerness in all its highs, lows, with all its heroes, heroines and occasional villain, with its moments to remember, moments of triumph, moments of reflection, but ultimately a celebration of those to be proud of, those who let the world know their truth, and who will never be forgotten because of it. We hope you enjoy using and perusing it as much as

we loved creating it.

Robert Barber

John Callaghan

Tanya Wischerath

APPLICATIONS OF THE MODERN QUEER TAROT

I wouldn't presume within the pages of this book to instruct someone as to the right or wrong way to use a tarot deck. All I can do is say what works for me, what feels right for me, what my lessons and initiations in the use of the Tarot were, what informed and still informs such lessons, and why it all has remained true and unwavering for me to this day. I was lucky enough to be taught by Tarot practitioners (one of whom was to me most certainly a magus of and with the cards) who approached it as much a science as anything else and relied less on intuition as memorization of the age-old definitions and divinatory meanings of the cards.

Intuition becomes an important aspect of a reading once the foundation is laid, once it is obvious what the spread is about, clarity as to what questions are being asked, what is at the heart of the matter at hand, and where the answers may lie. Intuition should kick in when looking for the connections *between* the cards; it has no place in deciphering what the cards mean themselves individually. In fact, the intuition of the reader (the one interpreting the cards) matters less than the intuition of the querent (the one for whom the work is being done). When the reader asks the querent what comes to their mind after the meanings of cards are explained to them, *that* is the intuition that needs to be paid attention to. The reader must probe and ask and put those connections together, for the querent is likely distracted by the thoughts and images coming to their minds after the cards are explained. In some ways, the querent's sensitivity, psychic ability, and feelings about the cards come into play and matter more during a tarot card reading than those of the reader. It's the reader's needed intense and well-studied knowledge of each card, and how those cards react to each of the other seventy-eight, that the querent is relying on to give them the best interpretation that can be gleaned from the spread at hand.

Hence, the scientific approach to the Tarot I mentioned earlier that I was taught when I first started. The sensitivity or intuitiveness that many believe is needed to become a great or even good tarot card reader can come to anyone who *believes* that they are highly sensitive and intuitive. For me, I ask that you *learn* the cards. Learn their meanings, and their correspondences. Learn the elements and their properties. A good knowledge of astrology is a boon to being a tarot card reader, and can't be understated. Learn what cards attract repel and one another. This is the way to become a great tarot card reader. The joy, wonderment and awe you'll feel once you reach that threshold, when you can use a deck and understand the fractal dimension-like potential that the seventy-eight cards hold in their relationships with one another.

The layout I've used most often in my life is the fifteen-card spread made famous by Aleister Crowley in his celebrated, arguably unsurpassed Thoth Deck. As stated in the booklet that accompanies that deck to this day, the spread is indeed "rapid and reliable". The 'X-spread' as I've always called it, as the five placements of three cards each resembles an 'X' when done (although it also looks like the five dots for a number '5' on a die), is what I was taught, along with the long-classic Celtic Cross, a ten-card spread that is probably as old as the oldest decks. On very rare occasions, I attempt what is called a Platinum Spread, where you use the entire deck (hence Platinum, as its atomic number is 78), creating thirteen columns of six cards, with each column representing changes, events, and people in the coming twelve months; the final column being the qualities and unavoidable fates the querent should adhere to and/or embrace for the best outcome.

The Platinum Spread is always a daunting exercise and

requires hours of questions and study with the querent, often needing the reader to spend several days alone with the cards, interpreting them very carefully. Like the Platinum Spread, The X-spread relies utterly on the relationships of the cards to one another in achieving an accurate interpretation. And as with Crowley, and many other readers and decks that came and went both before and after him, I've never used *reversed* meanings. I find the notion of 'direction' too arbitrary a reason to interpret a card as negative, opposite of, or ill-dignified towards its accepted meaning. It makes much more sense, as well as being poetry to me, to find that the flow of love and happiness that fills many a Cups card is stifled by the choke of a malignant Wand. Or that the lifting hope brought by The Star is tangled and laden by an abundance of Coins.

I tell the querent to shuffle the cards at least three times, beforehand asking them to think of the issue or issues they'd like addressed, questions they want answered, etc. I also ask them to imagine a flow of energy coursing from their brain, down their arms and into the cards while shuffling. It very often can feel like tingling, tickling accompanied by a popping of the ears and/or goose bumps on the arms. I also find that it's important for silence during the shuffling. I let them shuffle as long as they like, as long it's at least three times. I then take the cards from their right hand and lay them out as follows (The X-Spread), in the order from one to fifteen:

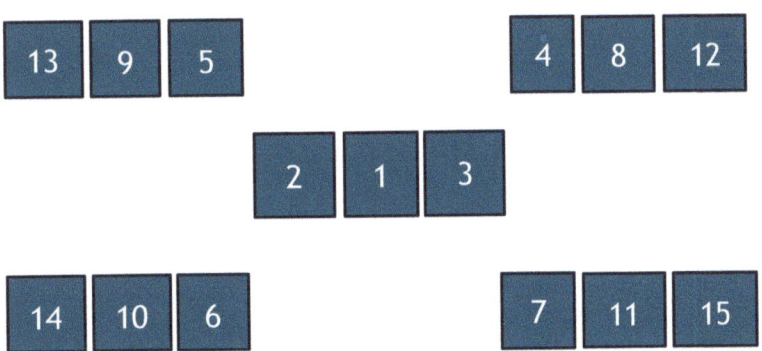

Turn all the cards over at once before any interpretation is said. Look right away for an abundance of Major Arcana, as this will foretell a significant reading, one with a major impact on the querent's current situation in life. Also, look for a profusion of one or two elements over the others, as this may herald great conflicts restricting, or great support towards, the actions the spread recommends, depending on the relationship between said elements. (Many huzzahs to the Thoth Deck for the following position/placement definitions)

Position #1: This stands in for the querent themselves. It describes the situation at hand and the main weight or authority at sway.

Positions #2 & #3: These are added descriptors for the card in Position #1. They provide clarity, depth, color, location and temporality of the situation at hand.

Positions #4, #8 & #12, as well as **#5, #9 and #13** provide two distinct possibilities. Think of them as a fork in the road. If all six cards complement one another, or rather, if there's no conflict to be found amongst them, then the three on the upper right are the path to take, with the cards on the upper left there to help guide, assist, providing precision and a closer inspection of what's at hand. If they are not complementary to one another and there's friction between the two triads, or within them, then the cards on the upper right are an inevitability unless action is taken.

In this case, then the cards on the upper left provide an alternative, or at least clues as to how to avoid the oncoming. In the case where the two triads are in conflict with each other, but you want the upper right to happen, then the upper left are a warning, describing what will try to throw you off course.

Positions #6, #10 and #14 are there to assist the querent in whatever decision-making is needed anywhere throughout the spread. They're often reminders of why the querent is asking the questions at hand to begin with, what brought them here, and what not to forget; they are either the immediate past, what's recently been resolved, and/or recent lessons learned to be remembered.

Positions #7, #11 and #15 inform the querent of powers, institutions, situations, people, systems, and forces, to which they have no choice but to acclimate to. These are things beyond the control of the querent and should be seen as the greatest of advice.

I hope this bit of instruction infused with a little history of my Tarot beliefs and pedagogy helps in some way to start you off on the great personal adventure with your own deck. Tarot cards are rooted in centuries-old symbols, myths, correspondences, attributions, stories, esoterica, harmonies, claims, truths, sciences, poetry, and religions, that should be esteemed to a high extent, and if altered and personalized, done so without appropriating them and amalgamating them to the point where the cards become unrecognizable as Tarot. I'm hopeful that with the Modern Queer Tarot, we've honored those words, that we've created something that is utterly respectful to its seemingly ancient tradition, but looked at from another angle, infused with my own sensibilities, making it not something other than tarot, but perhaps something further.

FIRE	WATER	AIR	EARTH
All the Wands	All the Cups	All the Swords	All the Coins
The Emperor	The Priestess	The Fool	The Empress
Strength	The Chariot	The Magician	The Hierophant
Fortune	The Hanged Man	The Lovers	The Hermit
Temperance	Death	Justice	The Devil
The Tower	The Moon	The Star	The Universe
The Sun	Judgment		

Robert Barber

THE MAJOR ARCANA

THE FOOL

The Fool is the tarot card that stands on its own – it holds no universally accepted position within the deck. Some will argue that The Fool is the beginning of the deck (the far most common view), some say the end, some say both the start *and* the end, and even some that it lies completely outside the deck. Often, it is helpful to think of The Fool as the center of a wheel, and the other twenty-one cards as the spokes which come from it, or lead to it, depending on your perspective. There are worthy arguments to have it be attributed to the number zero and also to the number twenty-two. In addition, The Fool symbolizes or stands in for you, the querent, the one asking of the tarot, the traveler who navigates through the lessons of the other twenty-one cards of the Major Arcana.

The Fool's here to seek experience, to stir agitation, to give a name to the unknown, to signify a liminal state, and possibly to prolong it. The Fool is liberated, or rather, has never been truly bound to anything. It's nascent, primeval and chaotic as an electron; just when you think you've figured The Fool out, it has changed direction, moved on, transcended to the next plane, the next location, the next reaction – spreading an environment of peculiarity and audacity. Think of it as attempting to perpetuate a world where nothing is ever perpetual save its own unpredictability. It desires the primordial, the new, the young – the truly un*adult*erated. It doesn't seek out danger, but what it's attracted to is often just dangerous. The Fool is tomorrow's ethic, and today's wickedness. The Fool sees what it sees and feels what it feels without thinking, but it's a purposeful 'non-thinking'.

Interpretively, The Fool can mean anything from sudden, severe change, to the birth of an original idea; from recklessness in and restlessness of the present state, to the desire for new experiences; from manic to suddenly carefree and devil-may-care. Almost more than with any other card in the deck, The Fool's divinatory meaning is influenced by what's around it, for The Fool is an innate blank slate. *Where* in your life The Fool's qualities will be felt depends on the attributes and correspondences of neighboring cards in the spread. Similarly, whether it's the Fool's welcome eccentricity or its warped craziness that will rear its head is similarly dependent on the cards around it.

The Fool is a card of the element of Air, being ruled by Uranus, the planet of Aquarius (an Air sign), and therefore its most beneficial aspects emerge when near Swords, or other Air-based Major Arcana. When near Wands and Cups, or Fire and Water-based Major Arcana, interpretation of The Fool's effects are likely positive, but care should be taken to reign in its wild spirit when its work of reordering and reapplying is done. If its placement is near Coins or Earth-based Major Arcana, The Fool's chaotic influence is at its most malignant – beware of bodily harm and/or economic downturns.

Jean Genet (1910 – 1986) Influential 20th Century French novelist, dramatist, poet and critic.

Genet's mother was a prostitute who sent him to provincial France for adoption. Once there, he became a 'problem child', prone to stealing, running away and other petty crimes. At fifteen years old, Genet was sent to the notorious Mettray Penal Colony, later a focal point of Foucault's (The Universe) masterwork *Discipline and Punish*. Upon leaving there at eighteen, Genet joined the Foreign Legion only to be kicked out when he was caught having sex with another man. He then survived by hustling and stealing his way across Europe.

From these raw and visceral experiences, Genet fashioned a series of uncompromising novels (*Querelle of Brest, The Miracle of the Rose*) and plays that were revolutionary in their graphic portrayals of male homosexual desire in the previously dark corners of French society. Genet inverted traditional moral values, celebrating criminality and betrayal, and sanctifying queer desire. Genet not only homo-eroticized the degraded, he also elevated them spiritually.

Genet lived the life of a petty criminal and prostitute before eventually elevating and consecrating these qualities within his art, thereby forever changing the way we perceive the least-integrated margins of society.

Genet exemplifies The Fool through his singular, constant identification not only with the outsider, and with the constant, protean aspects of existence, but also with his reversal of conventional morality. Genet transformed his *fool*-ish experiences into genius rather than madness (mostly); his journey from vagabond to artist, from transgressor to saint, *is* the journey of The Fool.

0

THE FOOL

THE MAGICIAN

The Magician is the card of decisive mental action. Taking the first clear and logical step towards the new design and enterprise hinted at in The Fool, The Magician is a jolt of consciousness, an initial awareness that eventually leads to denser and more complex thoughts and states (the remaining cards of the Major Arcana). With The Magician arises notions of aptitude, focus, language, perception, and precision – an awakening of the left-brain. Whereas The Fool is the suggestion of change, the desire and need for it, The Magician *is* the change itself, the first trigger and charge of a new idea, a new expression – the subconscious brought into consciousness. The moment flint touches steel is The Fool; the spark is The Magician. There's nothing The Magician can't do – its confidence is supreme, unrivaled, and untouched.

The keywords to remember about The Magician are *skill* and *intellect*. The Magician will help you make a decision, move with clear direction, know what to do, recognize your powers and gifts and get on the path towards their greatest realization/utilization. There is a boundless light in this card that is emanating from your self-awareness, your ego, the confident belief in the new idea of The Fool, and the great potential this brings. The Magician also makes everything go smoothly, as it has the talent to be thorough, and to go through, around and over any plain and obvious obstacles in the path.

As its ideas are clearer and sturdier than anyone else's, The Magician's appearance helps you win every debate, often by synthesizing the old ways into the new, for only by fully understanding what came previously can you create what needs to be. There is no shame in being correct, particularly when it comes from a comprehensive, pedagogical source. The Magician knows this, and its power should be pushed forward whenever it rears its head. However, be careful not to get carried away by this burst of self-esteem and power – it can interfere with sound judgment.

The Magician is also, like The Fool, a card of the Air, albeit ruled by Mercury, the planet of Gemini (an Air sign). Therefore, it's most beneficial when supported by Swords, or other Air-based Major Arcana. When near Wands or Cups, or Fire and Water-based Major Arcana, interpretation of The Magician's effects are still positive, we just need to make sure you're not imposing your will on others, that your character isn't driving the plot forward without anyone else's input or viewpoint, that you're not

sucking all the air out of the room. If its placement is near too many Coins or Earth-based Major Arcana, The Magician is prone to deceptions and crime, all done in the name of achieving goals. The Magician's dark side is the malignance of utilitarianism.

Susan Sontag (1933 – 2004) American essayist, critic and novelist.

Susan Sontag was one of the great public intellectuals of her time. Known for her erudition and searing intelligence, she shifted the focus of Western philosophical discourse, sometimes onto queer themes.

Sontag's brilliance manifested itself early in her life. She graduated high school at fifteen years old and went on to study and socialize with many highly regarded academics in the U.S. and Europe, including Iris Murdoch and Allan Bloom. Sontag is perhaps most famous for her 1964 essay "Notes on Camp" (originally published in her 1966 debut collection *Against Interpretation*), a high-brow cultural critique of the low-brow style of entertainment loved by generations of queers everywhere. Her later work, *AIDS and Its Metaphors*, turned the spotlight on how language ("plague", "high-risk groups", "deviant") stigmatized people with AIDS.

Sontag was heavily criticized throughout her illustrious career, notably for her activism during the siege of Sarajevo, which was considered overbearing and self-indulgent, and her American-imperialism comeuppance stance on the 9/11 attacks. She also managed to alienate all sides in her negative assessments of both Western culture *and* the Communist alternative. Most of Sontag's romantic relationships in life were with women, most notably the famed photographer Annie Leibowitz, but having come of age in the era of "open secret" bisexuality or homosexuality, Sontag didn't fully, or rather, publicly, come out until a 2000 *Guardian* interview.

Susan Sontag exemplifies The Magician because she was generally the smartest person in the room, the one leading the discussion, and the one who showed us new ways of seeing and understanding. Her genius in using rational thought to synthesize vast amounts of information into original insights, and in being able to isolate objective truths and use them to reshape perceptions by the sheer force and skills of her intellect *is* the transforming power of The Magician.

THE MAGICIAN

THE PRIESTESS

The Priestess is the card of intuition, tranquility and repose. Offering a different path of manifestation than the one offered by The Magician, The Priestess takes the idea set off by The Fool and puts instincts and feelings to work. With The Priestess arises calm appreciation, introspection, inference, empathy, and stillness – an awakening of the right-brain. The Priestess is also the first mother, the mother of forms, and it rules over giving your new ideas, as well as their accompanying hopes, an emotional, yet tangible, shape. The Priestess wants you to truly *examine* your personal relationships, to check in with yourself and make sure there's a proper balance between love, work, and play – it wants you to remember that you are your other's other: be it that 'other' is a family member, partner, friend, community, countrymen, or humanity itself. The Priestess wants you to see yourself through others' eyes; it can be construed as subjectivity incarnate.

The Priestess doesn't *know*, rather, it *understands*, and it is through this complete, almost serene understanding that The Priestess works its magic. It is the master of concentration as well as contemplation, making its judgments all the more sound and exalted. The Priestess is telling you that the answers you seek are to be found through a version of self-work (as in working on the self), being alone, quiet, and often with nothing more than common sense as a guide. It knows that you know right from wrong, and it wants you to have the desire to do what's right for its own sake. There is a humanist optimism in The Priestess that can be taken as a mother always loving and expecting/hoping for the best in and of their children; you are, and at all times, either the child of action or of intuition, a child of The Magician or The Priestess. The appearance of The Priestess in a spread reminds you to listen to your conscience, inner voice, and dreams, and to go with your gut, not in the sense of being brave or courageous, but rather in the sense of doing the right thing, which most already truly know prior to contemplation.

The Priestess is a card of Water, ruled by The Moon, who in turn rules Cancer (a Water sign). Therefore, it's most beneficial when supported by Cups or other Water-based Major Arcana. When near Swords or Coins, or Air and Earth-based Major Arcana, interpretation of The Priestess' effects are still positive, but you just need to make sure you're not led away by enthusiasm, or that your new revelations aren't shallow and insincere. If its placement is near too many Wands or Fire-based Major Arcana, The Priestess is an omen for conspiracies, harmful gossip, and/or the divulgence of damaging and dangerous secrets.

Virginia Woolf (1882 – 1941) English writer famous for portraying the interior thoughts and feelings of her characters; for the 'stream of consciousness'.

Born and educated in a liberal, highly artistic family (her father, Leslie Stephen, being the first editor of the *Dictionary of National Biography*, and her mother, Julia Duckworth, a muse and model for both Edward Burne-Jones and Julia Margaret Cameron), Woolf displayed a sensitive temperament early on. Throughout her life, she suffered a series of nervous breakdowns, often followed by periods of depression and was institutionalized on a least three occasions; she most likely suffered from bipolar disorder, a diagnosis not available at the time. Woolf, along with her husband Leonard and sister Vanessa Bell, was a member of the Bloomsbury Group – a clique of intellectuals and artists famous for not just their formidable talents but also their pranks, and liberal attitudes to sexuality.

Woolf's novels are frequently listed among the best fiction of the twentieth century. She is also regarded as a pioneer of not only Modernism and feminist writing, but also of homosexual desire.

Her marriage to Leonard Woolf was emotionally rich and mutually supportive. In late 1922, she met Vita Sackville-West (Nine of Coins), with whom she had a loving, romantic relationship lasting many years. Virginia wrote the novel *Orlando* for Vita, a story in which the main character ceases aging, changes sex and proceeds to live a remarkable life through three turbulent centuries.

When she turned fifty-nine, Woolf felt her old demons returning. Unwilling to face them again, not wanting to be a burden on her husband and sister any longer, and suffering from the singular depression brought about by the doom and destruction of another World War, she filled her pockets with stones and walked into the River Ouse near her home in Sussex, drowning herself.

Virginia Woolf exemplifies The Priestess because her writings emphasize interior, affective states – the important action being *inside* the character. She explores the richly intuitive sense of a situation and places feeling above rationale or logic as a way of experiencing the world.

II

THE PRIESTESS

THE EMPRESS

When you reach The Empress, we encounter a card of astonishingly singular supremacy, as you will again with The Emperor. No other card in the Tarot typifies fecundity, gentleness and the sheer declaration of life as simply and powerfully as The Empress.

With this card arises sensual pleasure, sexual delight, ease, and the finding of beauty and exquisiteness. Unlike The Priestess, whose motherhood is a perpetual potential, a "Virgin Queen," if you will, The Empress is a constant mother through and through. Pregnant with all life, The Empress is forever in the act of birth – reminding you that renewal is always a possibility no matter what the situation might be, no matter how bleak, no matter how dead. Whether the previous path was one of rational thinking (The Magician) or intuition (The Priestess), The Empress augurs a rich fruitfulness and the nurturing aspect of all new ideas.

The Empress delights not only in partaking of the splendor and enchantment of the sensual world, but also in believing and recognizing Spirit's ubiquity in all creation; it sees the two as essentially the same thing. The appearance of The Empress in a spread heralds earthly and material successes, creative fertility, and/or an abundant output from dreams and the subconscious. There is also great passion in this card, as The Empress, for all its reveling in the state of growing and love, is still a card of profound, almost possessive, intensity.

This intensity can be all-consuming and paralyzing, as it demands a complete and total surrender to grace, something few can ever achieve in this day and age. Ultimately, it is a card of bounty, and pure, true satisfaction. There's the greatest of joys in birth, whether it be of an idea, a relationship, a work of art or craft, or the birth of life itself. The Empress proclaims an actual, feasible beginning. The seeds have sprouted, and the nurturing has begun, but soon the physical, laborious work (the molding, the teaching, the instruction) will commence, as will the lessons of compromise and ego.

The Empress is a card of Earth, ruled by Venus, who in turn rules Taurus (an Earth sign). Therefore, it's most beneficial when supported by Coins, or other Earth-based Major Arcana. When adjacent to Wands or Cups, or Fire and/or Water-based Major Arcana, The Empress is still a card of great boon, providing authentic, rich grounds for art and love to prosper, but be careful of being dragged into dissipation and debauchery (an excess of Cups), or idleness (an excess of Wands). If The Empress' placement is near too many Swords or Air-based Major Arcana, it exudes coldness, withholds love, and paralyzes growth.

Walt Whitman (1819 – 1892) American poet famous for his unsurpassed free verse epic, *Leaves of Grass*.

Whitman's poetry celebrates the human spirit, and the promise of early America. Whitman is *the* root poet of the American psyche with his boundless enthusiasm for engaging with the glorious potential of a still-new country.

Born into a poor Long Island family, Whitman received little by way of formal education. He held jobs as a teacher, journalist, government clerk and civil war nurse. Whitman self-published *Leaves of Grass* in 1855; a work he would continuously revise throughout his life. Early positive reviews by notables such as Ralph Waldo Emerson were followed by reviewers who focused on the 'obscene' nature of some of his poetry. The Calamus poems, a sequence within *Leaves of Grass*, trace a relationship between the poet and his male lover as they sing the homoerotic joys of comradeship.

Truly democratic as well, Whitman's poems sing the songs of the masses and elevate the everyman. He believed that honest toil would bring the world's bounty and full potential into being. As well as being a devout deist, Whitman believed contradictorily that God was both immanent in all parts of the material world as well as transcendent of it. He also believed the human soul was not only immortal but in a constant state of development, productiveness and improvement.

Whitman exemplifies The Empress through his unabashedly sensual celebration of abundance and the expansive spirit of the world. He finds joy, pleasure, beauty and growth in everything he sees – and he sees everything, warts and all. His poetic eye ranges across the North American continent, through pastoral scenes, industrial manufacture, natural beauty, daily commerce, and always, the love between two people.

THE EMPRESS

THE EMPEROR

The Emperor is a card of implacable control, authority, and responsibility. It is here where you experience the first and purest ideas of discipline, paternal dominion/love and the imposition of will. With The Emperor arises the urge to conquer others, to enshroud them in the established hegemony; it is an incredible surge of active energy and male power. Unlike The Magician, whose power is that of expansive ideas, the free flow of thought and personal expression, The Emperor's is conservative, and focused on maintaining order, accommodating the superego, and using strife to quell strife: to fight fire with fire. It builds and imposes stability in chaotic situations. Structure is key to The Emperor, and very often in life its skill is needed and necessary. For better or worse, the roads The Emperor walks are paved with good intentions.

The Emperor has no qualms about being combative with another, or creating conflict to achieve the victory necessary. It signifies lawfulness, taking command of a situation, and/or the need to keep control. There is great inflexibility with The Emperor – it is a fundamentalist by nature and not fond of being compliant with external influences and forces. Therefore, you need to be wary of blind intolerance when The Emperor rears its head, for its presence can mean you fear opposition where there is only difference.

Otherwise, be sure to actually heed its strengths, and make use of them as you can, for The Emperor's commanding energy and leadership experience are without rival. The Emperor heralds the desire within you to be the leader, to be right, to be in control. He will assist by any means possible in making your dreams and ideas bigger and better.

The Emperor is a card of Fire, ruled by Aries, who in turn is ruled by Mars (a Fire planet). Therefore, it's most beneficial when supported by Wands, or other Fire-based Major Arcana. When adjacent to Swords or Discs, or Air and/or Earth-based Major Arcana, The Emperor is still a positive force, as the cards around it will benefit from its ability to negate chaos, flightiness and poorly structured plans; however, be careful of the pride and imperiousness that can come from wielding The Emperor's power successfully. If The Emperor's placement is near too many Cups or Water-based Major Arcana, he is a disaster waiting to happen: full of despotism, rashness, ill-temper and a tyrannical misuse of power, especially towards those you care for and/or love, including yourself.

Yukio Mishima (1925 – 1970) Post-war Japanese writer, actor, and filmmaker.

Yukio Mishima fused traditional aesthetics with contemporary politics in a highly polemic and controversial way. His overtly stylized works explore death, power, and sexuality – ideas that were also central to his life.

Descended from an ancient samurai family, Yukio Mishima's childhood was spent in the care of an oppressive grandmother, who was a very strong early influence. A violent woman who considered herself part of the aristocracy, she isolated Mishima and gave him an elevated sense of himself through the family's name and legacy. Later, Mishima's father, a government official, used military-style discipline in his severe parenting. Although drafted during WWII, Mishima was rejected on medical grounds – a bad cold he had was misdiagnosed as tuberculosis.

Yukio Mishima's early works, *Confessions of a Mask* and *Forbidden Colors,* tell of a homosexual double life. These were partly autobiographical, as he was married with two children while being sexually active with men. Exceedingly prolific, Mishima produced 34 novels, 50 Noh and Kabuki plays and 25 collections of short stories. He was even considered for the Nobel Prize on several occasions.

Mishima venerated the traditions of Imperial Japan and evolved an idiosyncratic form of extreme right-wing Nationalism in which he criticized the Left as well as the by-then lame-duck Emperor. Calling for the overthrow of civilian government and the restoration of the Emperor's powers, he led a small group of private militiamen in a doomed coup attempt. After its obvious failure, Mishima immediately committed ritual suicide (seppuku).

Yukio Mishima typifies the card of The Emperor with his commitment to traditional social and aesthetic values and his recourse to physical force to implement and conserve stable and paternalistic power structures.

THE EMPEROR

THE HIEROPHANT

The Hierophant is the card of spiritual guidance. After receiving the maternal and paternal energies of, respectively, The Empress and The Emperor, The Hierophant enters the picture to instruct about the divine, and the divine's participation in all forms of experience. With The Hierophant arises persistence, fortitude, and education – an awakening to a way of wisdom beyond the heretofore experiences of self and parents and the results thereof. It is the *senex*, the great teacher, the "Wise Old Man" of Jung, who instructs from its own learned knowledge and deeply held beliefs onto and into the mind of the student. The Hierophant wants you to step back and honestly reexamine what you believe about the issue at hand. It wants you to stop, evaluate and make sure that your way of seeing and understanding couldn't be improved upon through opening up to new, or long-forgotten ways of perception.

The Hierophant, unlike The Emperor, isn't going to lead you to its goal of deeper understanding by forceful means or through physical intimidation. Rather, The Hierophant teaches you that struggling is unnecessary, as you're already part of something bigger than yourself whether you like it or not. It unites the microcosm with the macrocosm, showing you 'as above so below' and challenges you to engage in non-rational ways of knowing. In place of reason, it invites you to use instincts, imagination and creative associations. This card is also associated with the formalities and rituals of organized religions and mysticisms. This might mean benefiting from disciplined work on a proven spiritual path or, with a negative connotation, being stultified within a rigid tenet, by a Svengali, or a traditional social convention.

The Hierophant is a card of Earth, ruled by Taurus, who in turn is ruled by Venus. Therefore, it's most beneficial when near Coins, or other Earth-based Major Arcana. When adjacent to Wands or Cups, or Fire and/or Water-based Major Arcana, The Hierophant is still a card of great edification, providing numinous inspiration to the situations and ideas (other cards) that surround it, but be careful of being told what you want to hear (Wands), and also of the advice of zealots (Cups). If The Hierophant is near too many Swords or Air-based Major Arcana, it is dangerously dogmatic, full of persecutions and stultifying convention.

Harry Hay (1912 – 2002) High-profile activist and advocate against queer assimilation. Founder of the Radical Faeries.

Harry Hay had a long and distinguished career in left-wing and progressive politics. A one-time member of the Communist Party, he was an activist in the cause of workers' rights and against fascism. Later, he shifted focus onto specifically gay issues and was a founding member of the Mattachine Society, one of the earliest Gay Rights groups in the United States. He soon severed his ties with the Mattachines as they abandoned confrontational tactics. Harry was firmly anti-assimilationist, believing we should not try to pass or adopt heterosexual or straight-acting ways. Sexual diversity and queer behaviors were something he defiantly celebrated. He was critical of the way the mainstream gay community marginalized the drag and leather scenes and viewed all queer groups as part of a cultural minority.

In 1979, Harry Hay was one of a small group (along with John Burnside, Don Kilhefner, and Mitch Walker) who established the Radical Faeries – a loosely affiliated group of spiritually minded gay men who embraced spontaneous ritual and alternative forms of community. The Faeries became a spiritual counterculture conceived and born within the gay community. However, as the movement grew there were several conflicts within the leadership, with Hay being accused of power-tripping. Despite the Faeries' egalitarian ideals, Hay, as elder statesman, retained the power to eject participants with whom he disagreed.

Harry Hay, the Hierophant, is the wise old man of Queerness. He draws our focus away from the material world and shows us the value of community, compassion, and ritual. Hay's spiritual principles centered on non-assimilation, defense of the marginalized and oppressed, and freedom of speech - he had little to say on the nature of the Divine itself. However, he could sometimes be so rigid in the application of his principles that others perceived egoism and orthodoxy on his part.

THE HIEROPHANT

THE LOVERS

The Lovers, though it could also be called The Partners, is the first card in the deck in which more than one person is represented and involved. The previous cards could be interpreted as manifestations of the querist yourself: energies discovered, archetypes revealed. With The Lovers, another *person* posits itself within the path of your (The Fool's) journey, daring you to integrate an *other* into your life, and therefore to be open to inspiration, to new worlds offered, to new values, to the challenge of difference, and to the heart-racing possibilities and dangers of love and attraction. The Lovers is the introduction of someone in your life who is here to stay; either you let it in, let it become a part of you, and you of it, or else your whole journey could become derailed and stuck for an indefinite amount of time. The key is to accept the temperance, the changes and shifts of life, to welcome the layering on, the shedding of a layer of your ego, of your own self, the adding on of another's ego, the added depth. For this is not just altering who you are per se, but rather it is an enhancement – *go with the flow.*

The Lovers, unlike The Hierophant, isn't going to teach you based on its own life experience. Rather, The Lovers invites you to join forces together, to meet life's challenges and ever-changing colors hand in hand. It wants you to use your head as well as your heart in these things. Gemini rules this card, so intelligence, mental aptitude and correct choices based on such are of the utmost importance. There's sublime poetry here: the first thing you should do with the wisdom gained by The Hierophant is to use it towards the pursuit of finding/accepting love, recognizing beauty, and gleaning what pleasure you can from life. The card is asking you to emotionally *and* intellectually analyze yourself, your values, your situations, remove what's not needed, thereby making room for what wants to melt with you, into you, and to forever become a part of you. You then work towards molding the world into a better place to live, compromise by compromise.

The Lovers is a card of Air, ruled by Gemini. Therefore, it's most beneficial when near Swords, or other Air-based Major Arcana. When adjacent to Wands or Cups, or Fire and/or Water-based Major Arcana, The Lovers is still a card of inspiration and affection, telling you that going with your gut and intuition will lead to creative success (Wands), or that attraction, love and beauty will soon take a positive precedence in your life (Cups). If The Lovers is near too many Coins or Earth-based Major Arcana, it brings conservativeness, indecision, contradiction, the childish avoidance of responsibility, and/or shallow partnerships.

Eva Gore-Booth (1870 – 1926) & Esther Roper (1868 – 1938) Writers, suffragists, and labor activists.

Irish poet Eva Gore-Booth was twenty-six, and convalescing in Italy from a respiratory illness feared to be tuberculosis (but thankfully wasn't), when she met Englishwoman Esther Roper, an active and highly notable suffragist. Soon after, Eva abandoned her privileged lifestyle to be with Esther. Eva was the sister of Constance Markovitz, the Irish revolutionary leader, and was a dear friend of W.B. Yeats (who highly praised Eva's poetry), a frequent visitor to the Gore-Booth family estate, Lissadell House, in the west of Ireland.

Eva and Esther lived rich and happy lives together. They were very prominent in the women's suffrage movement, active in the British Peace Movement against involvement in WWI and worked for the abolition of capital punishment and prison reform. They established Urania, a magazine of progressive views on sexuality and gender. Both Eva and Esther were also devout vegetarians and animal rights activists, condemning vivisections. Following the 1916 Rising in Dublin, Eva led the campaign to reprieve her sister, Constance, and Roger Casement (Five of Swords), who had been sentenced to death. Esther was committed to Eva, caring for her in life and publishing her poetry after her death.

Eva Gore-Booth and Esther Roper lived a life of emotional harmony, love, partnership, and togetherness. As The Lovers, they submitted to their devotion and need for each other and shared their passions with the world.

THE LOVERS

THE CHARIOT

Although The Chariot can exhibit its qualities in several different ways, it is quite plainly the card of great self-expression and making your wants and needs known to those around you. After the realization of The Lovers, that the only life worth living is one in which you remain open to love (and all its potentials of change and inspiration), The Chariot gives you the drive and willpower to grab the reins of this latest manifestation of self, fine-tune it and put it to real work. When at its fullest, truest expression, The Chariot not only keeps you honest, and keeps you in control of your emotions, but those around you witnessing your new self-expression and ambition will find you reliable and respectable. The Chariot also keeps your eyes on the prize if and when you find yourself surrounded by those who bring you ill will and/or wish you failure.

The Chariot is, therefore, a card of victory and defiance. If it appears in a spread at a time when you're in the midst of a struggle or fight, although it's not a guarantee of success, it at least means that the fight will have made you a better and stronger person. You'll find that you're able to take heretofore difficult or opposing energies, forces, or circumstances and make them work to your advantage, and/or for the best for everyone involved. It's as if what you learned to do for yourself inwardly in The Lovers you are now able to do outwardly with The Chariot. Your resolve is strong at this point, and you'll be able to communicate your ideas and previously nascent beliefs and thoughts in a manner you've always hoped you could. Also, The Chariot can be a card of great stamina. Besides being ready to move full speed ahead, you're also ready to dig your heels in and put up a good fight. This is a card of successful plans and projects too, and if it appears when you're contemplating such, by all means you should go for it. The Chariot is an omen of triumph.

The Chariot is a card of Water, ruled by Cancer. Therefore, it's most beneficial when near Cups, or Water-based Major Arcana. When adjacent to Swords or Coins, or Air and/or Earth-based Major Arcana, The Chariot brings clarity and focus of thought, intellectual decisiveness (Swords), or good health and/or gaining recognition for hard work well done (Coins). If The Chariot is near too many Wands or Fire-based Major Arcana, it can be the harbinger of much discord. You should be careful not to resort to violence or manipulation in order to preserve your values or to achieve your goals. An ill-dignified Chariot can also bring a lack of control and confidence, and the possibility of failing to meet your own standards.

Quentin Crisp (1908 – 1999) Writer, actor, raconteur, and professional sissy.

Wearing makeup, nail polish and flamboyant clothes, the proudly effeminate Quentin Crisp was both stylish and shocking as he walked the streets of London's Soho working as a rent boy in the late 1920s and into the '30s. Far from the conventional suburban background into which he was born (as Denis Charles Pratt), he became famous for his contrarian approach to life and his witty way of expressing it. Explaining why he never did any house cleaning, he said, "After the first four years, the dirt doesn't get any worse".

He wrote an autobiography, *The Naked Civil Servant*, in which he described the regular humiliations, beatings and arrests he suffered during the first half of his life. The 1975 film version, starring John Hurt, brought Crisp and its star instant fame. Soon, Crisp was enchanting theater audiences as he languidly recounted his mad, colorful existence in a one-man show.

In 1981 he moved to New York, where he became a celebrity socialite, attending the best parties, knowing the best people, and being regularly quoted in the press. Crisp always kept his phone number listed and claimed he would accept a dinner invitation from anyone willing to pay – in return he charmed and entertained the other guests. Forever controversial, he famously criticized Princess Diana, calling her trashy, vulgar, open-eyed of everything, and no victim of the Windsors: "I always thought Diana was such trash and got what she deserved. She was Lady Diana before she was Princess Diana, so she knew the racket. She knew that royal marriages have nothing to do with love."

In the last year of his life, Crisp came to the realization that he was a trans woman instead of a gay man. He stated in letters published posthumously that had he the wherewithal and money when he was younger to have a sex-change operation; he most certainly would've gone through with it, a trans woman being what he felt he was and wanted to be all along.

Few have ever expressed themselves as uncompromisingly as Quentin Crisp. He proudly and willfully drove The Chariot through life, defying and queering the world as he went.

VII

THE CHARIOT

STRENGTH

Once you're off and running with The Chariot, the next step is to gauge your intensity and degree of self-expression. The Strength card is here to instruct you to either turn it up, be truly courageous, embrace your zeal and passion, to take the burst from The Chariot and now live life to the fullest, or to turn it down, using calm, compassion, and discernment towards the situation now confronting you. The best utilization of *strength* isn't always as a force to attack or to persuade, but instead as a defense, to be strong enough to withstand an onslaught, or to know when to rout. At this moment you're in control, so be confident, brave, and enthusiastic. You should pursue the love you desire, the cause you believe in, and have the will to take control of your life's path, but also have the wits to know when to back down, when enough is enough, and when you need to let others take the lead. Nevertheless, the Strength card is spontaneity and ardor; it is the current temporarily connecting human power with the divine powers – use it while it's here.

Another manifestation of Strength is the ability to understand and tolerate others' ideas, beliefs and actions. Having control over your reactions and emotions is an expression of great strength indeed, and this card's appearance can be a warning against losing your temper. Strength can mean taking the higher ground, giving people their space, and/or needing to rein yourself in before any real damage is done. If the card appears when you're confronted with making a difficult choice, trust that you'll have the ability to manage whatever obstacles arise after the decision is made.

Lastly, Strength is a card of finding joy in life's physical activities. You have energy and vigor for days now, for taking pleasure in what amuses you, what makes you happy, what makes you feel lusty and alive, regardless of the risk – for you know there really is none at this moment.

Strength is a card of Fire, ruled by Leo. Therefore, it's most beneficial when near Wands, or other Fire-based Major Arcana. When adjacent to Swords or Coins, or Air and/or Earth-based Major Arcana, Strength also brings added patience and serenity (Swords), or the ability to remain carefree and childlike amidst adversity while maintaining control and responsibility (Coins). If Strength is near too many Cups or Water-based Major Arcana, it can be reduced, corrupted, bringing prejudice, selfishness, and egotism. Nothing will be good enough, and/or your tyrannical behavior will lead to shame and scandal.

Bayard Rustin (1912 – 1987) Humanitarian, socialist and civil rights activist.

With his core beliefs in non-violence and civil disobedience, Bayard Rustin was a central figure in the American civil rights movement and a close ally of Martin Luther King, having refused to comply with Jim Crow laws related to seating on buses thirteen years before Rosa Parks. He was also extremely active within the labor movement and, in later life, became a voice for gay rights.

Raised a Quaker, and continuing to practice as one throughout his life, Rustin travelled to India in 1948 to learn the non-violent protest and civil disobedience techniques of Mahatma Gandhi from the leaders of the Gandhian Movement and was subsequently arrested many times for his own peaceful protests once back in the States. He was recognized as a brilliant strategist, putting his talents to ultimate use as the main organizer of the 1963 *March On Washington*. Rustin also led the desegregation of labor unions. In 1986, he prophetically stated that gays had replaced blacks as the "barometer of social change".

In 1953, Rustin was arrested for homosexuality, and this forced outing (though he was long out of the closet privately) marked the trajectory of his career. He was labeled a pervert and an immoral influence by many of his peers in the civil rights movement, as well as by segregationists. Rustin was forced to take a back seat for the first time in his life and avoid public leadership roles. Until relatively recently he was grayed out of civil rights history. In 2013, President Obama awarded him a posthumous Presidential Medal of Freedom.

Powerful self-expression harnessed for a just cause and the wisdom to allow others to lead kept Rustin on a successful path. He was a powerful influence on the civil rights movement, with his dynamism and control in using non-violent tactics exemplifying the Strength card's poise and discipline.

VIII

STRENGTH

THE HERMIT

After so much passion, motion, and energy at play, there comes a time when what you need to do is remove yourself from the situation at hand and begin a notable period of self-analysis. This is when and how The Hermit comes into your life, and when it does it's a wonderful thing indeed. The Hermit is ruled by Virgo, whose planet is Mercury – the planet of communication, messages, information, and intelligence. This is a perfect fit with The Hermit, as it wants you to be intellectually prudent, astutely circumspect, to use your wisdom alone in analyzing this part of your life, and to question everything around you. The Hermit also wants you to walk, to wander, to wonder, and go where you need to go to find the answers you seek. However, you need to be alone during this time, away from the world, away from friends and family, removed from participation in all things that require interaction with others. Even if retirement from the present isn't possible at this time, when The Hermit appears in a spread the desire to be alone should be acknowledged and worked towards.

You should try to be more introspective towards whatever issue in your life The Hermit is referencing, be it job, relationship, or situation. Learn to cultivate a degree of introversion in all this, without becoming too narcissistic. You should think critically about yourself vis- à-vis your place in the world, whether or not you're contributing as you should, or as you would wish to be. Don't share emotions, desires, or wishes with anyone right now – keep the world at arm's length.

When The Hermit appears, it could also be an excellent time to do some serious soul searching, by spiritual, philosophical or meditative means. There is a seed, an inner guide, an illumination within you that can be made grown, made manifest and/or incorporated into your life if you only take the time to step back and nurture it. There's an incredible opportunity here to achieve a kind of personal, unique perfection with anything you put your mind to, but again, as long as you put the time and the life into it.

As stated before, The Hermit is ruled by Virgo, which is an Earth sign, so The Hermit is best when near Coins or other Earth-based Major Arcana. Its only hostility is when it is near too many Swords, or Air-based Major Arcana, in which case it can bring about acrimony and jealousy of others' lives, as well as arrogance as a cover for insecurity.

When very ill-dignified, The Hermit will result in sensory numbness, sociopathy, isolation and/or utter withdrawal from society, often into a ruinous state of mental decay.

Greta Garbo (1905 – 1980) Enigmatic, iconoclastic and reclusive movie star.

One of the all-time great, classic film actresses, Garbo was best known for her mesmerizing beauty and powerful screen presence. Her natural eroticism and subtlety of expression gave her an exotic quality in the Hollywood of the 1920s and '30s. She captivated audiences in a string of classic roles, including *Flesh and the Devil*, *Queen Christina*, *Camille*, and *Ninotchka*. American Film Institute has ranked her fifth on the list of greatest female stars of all time.

Garbo was born in 1905 in Stockholm, Sweden. Her family was working-class and truly impoverished, even for the time they lived in. Her father was a victim of the Spanish flu in 1919, leaving her to fend for herself. At the age of fifteen she was modeling and working in commercials, taking acting classes at night when she had the money and time. By 1925, she was in the States under contract to MGM, and by 1929, she was the biggest star in the world.

In 1941, aged thirty-five and with twenty-eight films under her belt, Garbo abruptly retired. Her persona had always centered on her desire "to be alone" – throughout her career she didn't sign autographs, very rarely gave interviews and never showed up at opening nights or awards shows. In her retirement she withdrew almost completely – spending her time exclusively with a close coterie of friends. She enjoyed walking the streets of New York, almost daily, hidden behind a heavy coat and large pair of dark glasses. She never married, had no children, and often spoke of her deep sense of melancholy. However, her letters reveal romantic relationships with several women, including Mercedes de Acosta (Five of Cups), as well as confidences with friends about her bisexual preferences.

Private, self-reflective, and always circumspect, Garbo withdrew from the hubbub of international stardom to focus on her interior self. As The Hermit she favored walking the streets anonymously, sifting through her melancholy and searching for the interior truths that yield real self-knowledge and inner perfection.

IX

THE HERMIT

FORTUNE

The wheel of Fortune is forever spinning in the background of your life. This random play of luck can come to the fore at any moment, altering and modifying everything in an instant, for better or for worse. Change is the only true constant, which means chance and opportunity constantly surround us. Whether or not you have the energy, wit, wisdom, or courage to seize the chance at hand is what Fortune is ultimately about. Not unlike The Lovers, the first card to represent something outside of the self (*the other* outside the querent), Fortune is the first card in which events (*the world* outside of the querent) affect your decisions, courses and outcomes.

Fortune heralds a change for a potential better, showing you where your best prospects lie, where/when you can turn your life towards a rewarding purpose, and how to take control of the traits, instincts and emotions that can turn an opportunity into a successful reality. Fortune pulls back the curtain and shows you an opportunity you may seize (or not). It's the fork in the road, the side passage that can be a shortcut, or maybe a longer path, but a chance nonetheless that could mean a windfall, a treasure to be discovered, an expansion. That being said, even ill-fortune can yield benefits if you address it correctly. Although there is no guarantee that your courage will result in an advantage or a boon, *never* taking a chance will always lead to worse outcomes, no resolutions, or even worse, the realization or suspicion that you missed an opportunity that would have led to a better life, that would have gotten you out of your rut.

The appearance of Fortune in a spread can also mean that current happiness, contentment and success can continue as long as you stay as you are and allow your daring and nerve to hold out. Good fortune and material well-being can go on, provided you avoid stasis, narrow-mindedness, or selfishness. Fortune's message to 'go for it' can also mean becoming physically active and embodied after a long-stretch of laziness and/or living your life too much in your head.

Fortune is ruled by Jupiter, which is in turn ruled by Sagittarius, a fire-based Sign, so it is best when near Wands or other Fire-based Major Arcana. It is hostile when near too many Cups, or Water-based Major Arcana, when it can point to utter emotional abandon. It warns against dangerous impasses brought about by ignorance, temper, and an unwillingness to change. An extremely ill-dignified Fortune card warns you of deep depression, negativity, and self-induced bad luck.

The Stonewall Rioters (1969) The public birth of the gay rights movement.

Police raids on gay bars were commonplace in New York's Greenwich Village (and in most, if not all, major U.S. cities) throughout the 1950s and '60s. In the early hours of Saturday, June 28th, 1969, the raid on the Stonewall Inn on Christopher Street started out as usual but quickly became a raucous riot when the queens and queers refused to do what they were told. Violence broke out, and the police, after much confusion, ended up barricading themselves inside the bar for their own safety as the crowd, grown to hundreds, found their collective courage, seized the moment and went for it.

Rioting continued throughout the day and into the next night and Gay Power was forever unleashed. Within two years, there were gay rights groups in nearly every major U.S. city, as well as Canada, Australia and Western Europe. Today, Gay Pride is generally celebrated at the end of June all over the world to commemorate the Stonewall Rioters.

Fortune favors the bold; the world would never be the same after the Stonewall Riots. It could have been just another police raid on a gay bar, but *Fortune*-ately it wasn't. The stranglehold of oppression and fear was broken because a bunch of queers and queens were tired of being pushed around and seized the opportunity to change things. Much could have gone wrong, but luck was smiling on them that night, and the wheel of Fortune spun in their favor.

FORTUNE

JUSTICE

Assessment in all its forms and possibilities is the key to understanding Justice and its appearance in a spread. Whatever position, state, circumstance, or period of your life you currently find yourself in, when the Justice card shows up it's best to heed its call for appraisal. Unlike The Hermit and its call to silence, to change through illumination from within, to bring about the variation yourself, with Justice, the adjustment is going to happen whether you like it or not. The lesson here is to learn how to reposition, rebalance and make the best decisions after the universe has had its way with you. Objectivity and wisdom always assist momentously when Justice's changes come along, as being able to see the bigger picture is optimal when it comes to the tools that help get you back on your feet. This card is saying that it's best to temporarily defer important action(s) until you've spent more time thinking about the issue/subject at hand. Precision and exactness are crucial here, as the wrong decisions now could lead to trials, lawsuits, miscommunications, and errors with a long period, if not a lifetime, of reverberations.

Expressions of empathy, honesty, and fairness are more than likely to pay off with Justice emotionally. Stop and look at all sides of an issue, where the other person, persons, or institution is coming from, and ask yourself if you're still correct or being reasonable. What feels like goading from another party might actually be your subconscious telling you you're in the wrong. This is also an excellent time to align yourself with another person, group, or cause.

When Justice appears it's trying to point you in the direction of a greater truth coming from within. There might be some unresolved issue from your past, or perhaps an entire aspect of life that you've ignored up until now (often the spiritual life in today's world), and Justice wants you to take advantage of these ignored truths. Seek them out, find out what you can take and use from them, and learn to make them balance within your own life. Justice isn't always the world crashing into you – it can also be you crashing into it.

Justice is ruled by Libra, an Air-sign, so it is put to its finest use when near Swords or other Air-based Major Arcana. The truly hostile side of Justice only appears when surrounded by too many Coins or Earth-based Major Arcana, in which case it brings about smugness, self-righteousness, unfairness and blatant dishonesty, often on a large scale. There is not only a severe failure to account for your actions, but a deliberate unwillingness to understand any cause, reason or concern other than your own – it is antipathy incarnate.

Oscar Wilde (1854 – 1900) Irish playwright, poet, novelist and wit.

Oscar Wilde was at the peak of his success in February 1895 when his life began to fall apart. *The Importance of Being Earnest* was playing in London to rave reviews, and Wilde had been and was still the toast of the town, celebrated for his creative genius, sharp humor, and extravagant lifestyle. His plays mocked the conservative attitudes and hypocrisy of Victorian England and elevated art and artistry above morality.

Wilde's relationship with the younger Lord Alfred Douglas, known as 'Bosie', was a loosely kept secret until the Marquess of Queensbury, Bosie's father, referred publicly to Wilde as a sodomite. Unwilling to let the insult pass, Wilde sued Queensberry for libel, against the best advice of friends and family. The salacious details of the trial were followed closely by the public. Queensberry won the case, and Wilde was quickly tried and found guilty of 'gross indecency', that is, of being gay. Imprisoned for eighteen months hard labor, Wilde became a social outcast following his release and died in self-imposed exile in Paris. His last work, the poem *The Ballad of Reading Gaol,* laments the brutality and demoralization of prison life.

Wilde's failure to assess the impact of the libel suit against a key figure in the British establishment, as well as his lack of objectivity and worldly knowledge, were his undoing. His unbalanced sense of the situation and inability to see things from others' perspectives caused him to collide with the world. Ultimately, Wilde's own poor decisions caused the weight of Justice to crush and destroy him.

JUSTICE

THE HANGED MAN

In order to move forward, to progress towards self-actualization, you must learn to abide suffering, accept eventualities (especially loss), and sacrifice. You must learn to give of yourself in ways you heretofore thought or felt to be near impossible/improbable, for fear of rejection, pain, or death. The Hanged Man is a card that is initially never welcome, but the upper hand can be gained through perspective. The submission and compromise it heralds are inevitabilities, so it's best to accept, invite in, and get a head start on making the best of the situation. When this card appears in a spread, look to its position, its precedence amongst the other cards, and what it neighbors. All these clues will help identify the area in your life where the 'letting go' must transpire. In matters of love (often when near Cups cards), The Hanged Man should always be welcomed, as its message of ego-subdual and giving of yourself can be an aid towards a successful relationship. There is a great spiritual awakening coupled with The Hanged Man too, one connected to the heart, emotions, and love, for only through pure vulnerability can the picture of self-knowledge become clearer. The Hanged Man itself tied the ropes that bind it, but only through a process of unencumbering can it again be free to walk the path of life.

The Hanged Man's appearance can also be a precursor of the need for a parental or teacher figure to help secure passage through this difficult time/decision. Reliance on those devoted to you, and to whom you are devoted, can help with this process. The suffering caused by sacrifice cannot be nullified, but leaning on loved ones for patience and understanding goes a long way. There is something to be said for the composure of The Hanged Man, for despite its predicament, it's never thrashing about in panic. It knows to remain calm and deliberate in the doing, and the undoing.

Lastly, the Hanged Man should be seen as a giver of wisdom, of clear realizations, of testing your ideas and beliefs so either *they* and you grow stronger (if they survive) or you alone do (if they don't). This warrants The Hanged Man's ability to change your perspective, for even when its trial is over we'll never forget the view from the hanging post.

The Hanged Man is ruled by Neptune, a planet of Water that in turn rules over Pisces, so the card is at its least disadvantage when near Cups or other Water-based Major Arcana. Tragically, when the Hanged Man appears in a spread near too many Wands or Fire-based Major Arcana, it will herald, at best, delays, indecisions, and petrification. When there's nothing nearby to aid its interpretation, the Hanged Man, when alight, brings punishment, martyrdom, defeat, failure, and utter rejection.

Alan Turing (1912-1954) British mathematician, cryptologist, and computer science pioneer.

Turing's contributions to the theory of artificial intelligence are considerable, and his notion of a Turing Machine is still widely used in the field. However, it was during the Second World War that he applied his genius mind to breaking the German enigma codes – used to send encrypted information to military units throughout the global battlefields. It has been estimated that the successful breaking of the German codes resulted in the war ending four years earlier than it might have otherwise. Alan Turing was a leader in this effort that saved countless millions of lives.

In 1952, Turing was convicted of 'indecency' when he reported a burglary at a flat shared with his lover, Arnold Murray. He pleaded guilty on the advice of his brother and his solicitor. To avoid a prison sentence, he accepted 'chemical castration' – a series of injections that destroyed his libido. He lost his security clearance and could no longer work at GCHQ (Government Communications Headquarters) on top-secret projects. Two years later, he committed suicide by eating a cyanide-laced apple. Finally, in 2017, the UK government retroactively exonerated all men convicted of 'indecency' in an initiative known as the 'Alan Turing Law'.

The Hanged Man endures suffering, and few have endured humiliation and exclusion as unjustly as Alan Turing. Sadly, his sacrifice did not result in resolution and deepened self-knowledge. Despite his huge contributions to humanity he was punished, martyred, defeated, rejected, and ultimately destroyed because of his sexuality.

THE HANGED MAN

DEATH

The person you are and the things you know come to die. Whether it's relationships with others, bonds with family and loved ones, what you believe in, how you define yourself, how you feel in/about the world, and even how you physically appear – all of these die.

More often than not, these aren't phases or even cycles of change, but complete and utter transformations. When the Death card appears in a spread, you should prepare yourself for one of these intense transitions. Everything depends upon how the card is situated in the spread (what it is near, how strong its presence is) in order to ascertain the nature and degree of the metamorphosis about to happen. Unlike other cards of change in the Tarot (Fortune, the Eight of Wands, or the Two of Coins, to name a few), the Death card is a momentous transformation. Although with Death, you simply have no choice in the matter – the wave is coming. You must give into it or settle for the petrifying stasis of the present (The Hanged Man). Whatever negative feelings you have about the change itself you must view it from an elevated perspective so that anger and resentment turn into positive driving forces: the tools to get through it.

This transformation can be eased into place by preparing its way and helping it along. This may sound odd or strange at first, but by assisting Death with its job you'll actually shorten the period of time it's around – the time the big change takes to settle. When compared to the sometimes slow speed of its own devices, this may be preferable. After death comes rebirth, and its possibilities are meaningful parts of life. Try to welcome them with open eyes and arms. Think of the times in your life when you felt that the changes that were coming, occurring, or just ending, were going to be too much, *were* too much, and how and when you wondered if you'd be able to face *that* day and the days to come. Nevertheless, you're here today. The pain is forgotten. The memory is smaller year after year. Remembering all this makes every appearance of Death that much easier as life goes on.

Rose-colored glasses aside, the appearance of Death in a spread can be an extraordinarily difficult time, full of heartache, consequences, endings, feelings of injustice, unfairness, and personal and spiritual betrayal. As with The Hanged Man, a sacrifice must be made, though not of a psychological or interior nature. Rather the sacrifice, the transformation, will be a large facet of your life, be it job, relationship, finances, health, status, and so on.

Death is ruled by Scorpio, a Water sign, so the card is at its least disruptive when near Cups or other Water-based Major Arcana. When Death appears near too many Wands or Fire-based Major Arcana, it's a warning against fears of, and resistances to, change and the refusal to grow out of old patterns and ways of being/believing. At its worst, Death heralds destruction through monstrous oppressions, cruelties and acts of violence. Death surrounded by Fire is a loss of soul.

ACT UP: AIDS Coalition to Unleash Power (since 1987) International direct-action group.

In 1987, AIDS was ravaging the gay community. Effective treatment options lay years in the future, and death stalked the bars and streets of gay neighborhoods in North America and Western Europe. It was a dark time with politicians ignoring the problem, drug companies seeking to profit, and the media still peddling fear. The gay community was in deep shock dealing with the crisis when American playwright Larry Kramer, frustrated by feelings of political impotence, urged queer New York activists to establish a direct-action advocacy group; two days later 300 people met and formed ACT UP.

In the years that followed, ACT UP smashed the putrefying inertia that had shrouded HIV/AIDS. They picketed Wall Street, stormed TV stations, protested the Catholic Church, and demanded action. They adopted and popularized the slogan **SILENCE = DEATH**, demanding a deep transformation in the way the Establishment responded to the AIDS epidemic.

AIDS brought death to many and unimaginably deep losses to many more. ACT UP transformed the anger, resentment, frustration and shock into positive driving forces; tools that got us through the crisis and ushered the rebirth of the gay community as an active force demanding change and shaping its own destiny.

DEATH

TEMPERANCE

There are moments throughout life when you recognize that you're composed of highly disparate forces, qualities, traits, or moods, sometimes extreme in contradiction. They can make you feel out of balance, lacking control, hypocritical, and/or pulled in opposite directions. Temperance is the card that recognizes and deals with these polarizing powers and intensities. After a big emotional or mental shake-up, a life-altering event or situation, you should always take stock, and chances are you'll find these opposing energies in front at play, or looming in the background. Perhaps you've just reached a point in your life where you're ready to confront either your personal hypocrisies, or, finally, do away with obsolete beliefs or ways of behavior/being.

This is a card of maturation, of shaking off what you don't need, of combining opposing or just different energies and forces, and weaving them into something new, workable and singular to ensure commonality. Position in a spread is crucial for all cards, but the importance of when and where Temperance appears cannot be overstated. Seemingly neutral and/or uncomplimentary cards now have a connector, a chance of resolution if Temperance is near. A unique and transcendent bridge can appear where once there was only chaos and confusion, or strange, alien, and seemingly unreconcilable surroundings.

Temperance can herald a moment of beneficial action resulting from skillful, accurate calculations, and success after planning; it can also bring about alliances that hold firm. Balance and coherence live where and when Temperance appears as well, and we can expect great satisfaction of mind, body, heart and spirit. This isn't a matter of replacing old with new per se, destroying one thing to be replaced by another; rather, Temperance can signify improvement and exaltation through synthesis, by being both things at once, and harmoniously.

Temperance is ruled by Sagittarius, a Fire-based sign, so it is at its most beneficial when near Wands, or other Fire-based Major Arcana. When near Earth or Coins, Temperance defines itself through economy, management, financial wizardry, or physical re-creation. When near Air or Swords, its purpose is obviously more mental and personal, bringing about new aspirations and meanings. Temperance can be negative when alone amongst Water or Cups. Its fire can be extinguished by gushy effusiveness, resulting in the opposing forces being taken to further extremes, tearing apart the issue at hand. This position heralds imbalance, excess and the loss of control.

We'wha (1849-1896) Celebrated Zuni *Lhamma,* weaver, potter, and acknowledged cultural ambassador.

Born in New Mexico in the same year that the Zuni people had their first contact with White settlers, We'wha was a 'two-spirit', or lhamana, as named within the Zuni. The Zuni, like many native groups throughout America, recognize more than two genders. They see beyond a simple male-female binary and celebrate the double-gendered as an honor bestowed by the Great Spirit with the power to intermediate between men and women. As a lhamana she was biologically a male who performed a hybrid social role, blending male spiritual functions with female domestic duties.

In 1877, White missionaries settled among the Zuni in an attempt to convert and assimilate them into Western culture. We'wha soon learned English and struck up a friendship with anthropologist Matilda Coxe Stevenson. She worked for Stephenson and shared a lot of information about their native culture. The instruction was not one-way – We'wha learned farming techniques from the settlers and taught them to the Zuni.

Achieving some fame, We'wha travelled to Washington D.C. and met President Grover Cleveland. While there, she demonstrated incredible weaving techniques with a backstrap loom, creating blankets, dresses and sashes. We'wha's renowned pottery was also shown in the National Museum in Washington, D.C.

We'wha successfully combined energies and forces of both the male and female aspects of Zuni culture to live with poise and harmony. She also balanced and blended native knowledge with new farming techniques learned from the missionaries. We'wha achieved what Temperance offers – improvement and exaltation through synthesis.

XIV

TEMPERANCE

THE DEVIL

It's vitally important to recognize and acknowledge when you're in possession of a great unchecked power. If left to its own devices, this power always corrupts, binds the soul to nefarious beliefs, and thwarts body, will and character from achieving the more sublime goals. As is often the case, this disreputable power is tied to the material world – your Self is desired, you have something someone wants, and you know the desires of others and use this knowledge against them. The twisted play between materialism and temptation, and between the ego and superego is the dark heart of The Devil card. It is an extremely male card, if not solely so, and is obsessed with corruption, amorality, the seven deadly sins, brutality and emotional detachment.

When The Devil appears in a spread, how it will manifest is dependent on those cards around it, because it attempts to debase them and bring out their worst. If you find yourself taking on The Devil's qualities then you must break free before it is too late and the damage to your soul too great. Recognition of personal responsibility is the first step in overcoming all harm, both to self and others. If The Devil is outside of you, manifesting as another person or persons, an institution, a system, then this will be a test of courage and willpower, a test of ameliorating the negative into the positive.

The Devil often heralds the arrival of an incredibly strong, somehow attractive and yet unscrupulous person. Again, this could be a side of yourself emerging, or another person altogether. Regardless, this manifestation hides behind ambition, hard work and endurance, which, although such a description may be accurate and real, it obscures the true purposes of domination, bondage, greed, and gluttony. Finally, The Devil is a warning against recklessness, moral blindness, and leaving things 'up to fate'.

The Devil is ruled by Capricorn, an Earth-based sign, so it's most transparent and conquerable when near Coins and other Earth-based Major Arcana. In such a case, The Devil makes itself known through physical temptations and brash violence – things easier to recognize as The Devil at work than, say, deception. If near Wands or Fire-based cards, The Devil seeks to corrupt the soul, leading to addictions, loss of faith/belief, and hence a loss of moral clarity. When influencing Cups or Water, it leads to tragic passions, rage, envy and painful, emotional dependency. Finally, and most dangerously, if The Devil is near too many Swords or Air-based Arcana, it can lead to fascist thinking, the death of empathy, severe mental instability and upheaval, and ultimately madness.

Roy Cohn (1927 – 1986) McCarthyite attorney and right-wing ideologue.

Born into a respectable New York Jewish family, Roy Cohn used family connections to get a job with the U.S. Attorney's office in Manhattan and quickly became a zealous prosecutor in the post-war, anti-communist witch hunts of the 1950s. Most famously he was part of the team that prosecuted Ethel and Julius Rosenburg for spying. Both were executed, although most evidence suggests that Ethel Rosenberg was innocent. He was also responsible for firing many government officials on the basis of suspected homosexuality during the Lavender Scare in the 1950s, despite himself being gay.

Unscrupulous in his private practice, Cohn's list of clients included mobsters and corrupt realtors, including Donald Trump; he even defended the Catholic Church against child abuse charges. Cohn also led a power grab for his family's business, Lionel Model Trains, from which he was later fired for incompetence.

Cohn was power-hungry and used his power to humiliate and ruin others. Like The Devil, lacking any moral compass, he allowed greed and self-interest to corrupt his soul and consume his life. For many, Roy Cohn will forever be remembered as played by Al Pacino in the TV version of Tony Kushner's *Angels in America*, dying of AIDS, alone and haunted by the ghosts of his own ugly past. Consumed with self-loathing, fear and hatred of others, he never made peace with his own sexuality.

THE DEVIL

THE TOWER

There are myriad kinds of change, both welcome and unwelcome: transformation, rebirth, sacrifice, rearrangement, adjustment, gain, ad infinitum. Destruction and disaster are also kinds of change, and The Tower heralds these particular moments. This could be a time of a pitched quarrel of words, a highly combative physical fight, or the beginning of a personal war. There is danger in The Tower, and you must be careful to avoid the falling stones and bolts of lightning that are bound to be projecting themselves in your direction. It is also a time to possibly admit defeat, assess and regroup if possible, or to let the survival instinct kick in and run for the hills.

The Tower is a very humbling card, for what you once thought was stable and secure now no longer is, and there is an unfortunate revelation in regard to weak foundations. When The Tower appears in a spread, look to what it is near, and heed its warning like no other card in the entire deck. Its ruin can be lessened or avoided if a clear path from other cards can be found; the cards that neighbor it are the aspects of our lives to be affected by its tragedy.

The Tower can have a positive spin if it comes into your life when you are actually yearning for the upheaval it offers, perhaps in order to get the new beginning you so desire, but are afraid to make happen yourself. The Tower sees neurotic and egoic forms and manifestations in your life as stains and blights, and seeks to eliminate them. It also provides an escape from the mundane order, the destruction of the old, and presents a ruin, yes, but also one that can be re-built upon, and with a radical perspective derived from having lived through a frightening experience. If cards of valor and determination are near, then The Tower is almost welcome if you're living an unhappy life. But be careful using The Tower this way, for its fire has a fallout that cleanses with no discrimination - its annihilation is perfect.

The Tower is ruled by the planet Mars, so it's a card of Fire, showing some benefit when near Wands or other Fire-based Major Arcana. In such cases (and also when near Swords or Air), The Tower destroys old ways of believing and/or seeing the world in order to lay the groundwork for a higher, more sublime philosophy or idea (Air) or belief (Fire). However, this can often manifest as smugness or fundamentalism. When near Coins or Earth, The Tower can mean fear of change, financial ruin, the destruction of plans, or a physical accident. If near Cups or Water, The Tower is particularly cruel, bringing about neurotic, dangerous neediness, a loss of great love, a renunciation, or a sudden death.

Francis Bacon (1909 – 1992) Anglo-Irish painter famous for his grotesque, tortured portraits.

Francis Bacon was one of the most famous painters of the 20th century. His most successful canvases show distorted figures caught in blurred, pitched screams, conveying the peak moment of inner torture and psycho-spiritual collapse. His central themes of crucifixion and physical corruption were perfectly in tune with the sense of angst and loss of personhood in post-war Europe.

Although Bacon was born into a wealthy Anglo-Irish family, he rejected the trappings of wealth and position for a bohemian, queer lifestyle. Attracted to working-class toughs, he fell in love with George Dyer, a petty criminal who he had caught breaking into his London flat. They had a violent, abusive, alcohol-fueled relationship lasting seven years. Dyer was uncomfortable among Bacon's intellectual friends and eventually committed suicide during Francis's hugely successful retrospective show in Paris. This resulted in an emotional and physical breakdown that Bacon channeled into the Black Triptychs, which are among his best-regarded works.

The Tower represents the complete collapse of an unstable situation - usually in a violent and chaotic way. Bacon's paintings seem to depict the pain and turmoil of the collapse of the Modernist worldview. His breakdown following his lover's suicide was like The Tower crumbling around him.

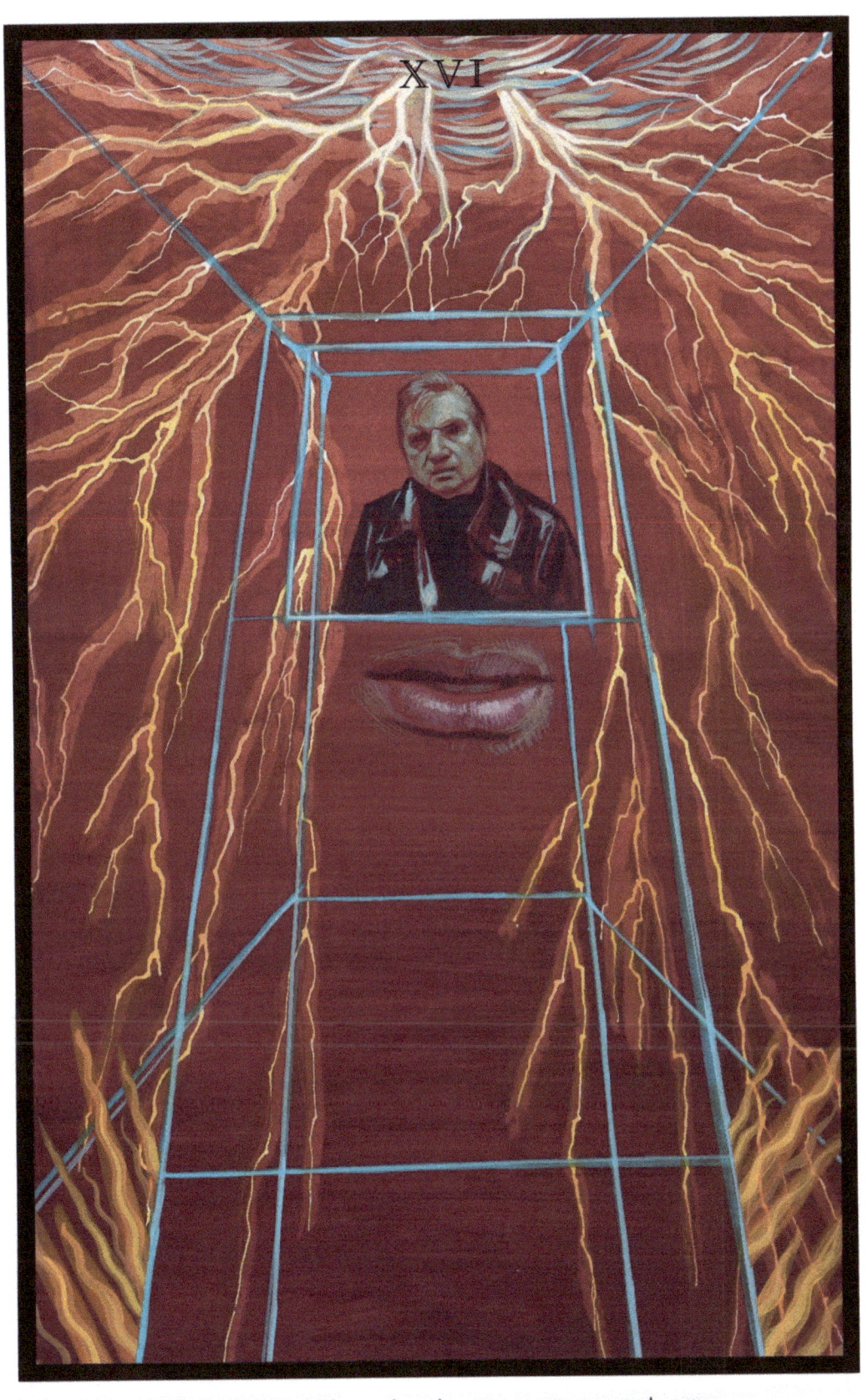

THE TOWER

THE STAR

Often after great strife and turmoil (The Tower) comes lucidity and freedom, a kind of enlightenment that arrives only from letting go of a defining fear or sorrow in your life. The Star signals a chapter of deep openness to love, hope, spirituality and calmness, and accessibility to hitherto unseen positive perspectives. Today, the quality of 'sensitivity' in your personality is too often seen as a weakness, at best called a trait of a passive nature. Yet sensitivity is a very powerful tool in discovering the commonalities of character in all humanity. The more you allow yourself to feel, the more you allow yourself to be seen in a 'state of feeling', and then the more those who observe you see what you share as human beings. Sensitivity and receptivity could perhaps be the saviors of humankind.

With this clarity comes not only enlightenment, but hope, acceptance, courage, and faith in a glorious future. When The Star appears in a spread, it has the power to blow away all clouds and smoke, mental hindrances, negativity, and aberrations of the soul. It takes a lot to block The Star, to keep it from shining bright even in the darkest of nights.

Like with the North Star, being under the influence of The Star card can feel like you're being guided toward your goal or destination. This may manifest, for example, if you're an artist, as a time in your work when you've come across astonishing inspiration, and/or the level or quality at which you're creating is something you've never experienced before. The notion of 'finding your true self' can begin with The Star. In extreme cases you may feel as if you're actually in contact with some kind of higher power, one that is really pulling the reins. Love is another important quality of The Star – some say it is the true card of love. The Star's appearance can herald a time in your life when you finally accept and believe others' or another's love for you, flaws and all. In your life this can be the most important revelation you can ever have.

The Star is ruled by the sign of Aquarius, so it's a card of Air, being at its most exalted when near Swords or other Air-based Major Arcana. The Star is the ultimate card to temper some of the worst qualities of the suit of Swords – it will assist and show the way through. Though of great benefit when near Fire and Water-based cards, beware of possible false prophesy with the former, and insensitivity with the latter. When surrounded by Coins or Earth-based Major Arcana, The Star can bring about erroneous judgment calls, over-confidence, wistfulness, or the inability to see life as anything else but labor and pain.

Harvey Milk (1930 – 1978) Openly gay American political leader, activist, and community organizer.

Elected to represent San Francisco's 5th District, which then included The Castro, on the city's Board of Supervisors in 1977, Harvey Milk was one of the first openly gay people to hold elected office in the U.S. Beginning as a grassroots community activist, he built alliances with labor and community groups and was soon known as the Mayor of Castro Street before being elected as City supervisor for the 5th District. He soon passed a gay rights ordinance outlawing discrimination based on sexual orientation. The gay rights movement had its first openly gay elected champion and hero. Only ten months later Harvey Milk was assassinated in his office along with Mayor George Moscone by Dan White, a conservative San Francisco Board supervisor for District 8.

White claimed diminished responsibility on the basis he had eaten too much junk food – the 'Twinkie Defense' – and was acquitted of murder. He was instead found guilty of voluntary manslaughter and given a reduced sentence for time served for good behavior. LGBT people were enraged at the injustice and marched to City Hall, where they stormed the building and burned police cars in what would become known forever as the White Night Riots.

Harvey famously said, "I know that you can't live on hope alone, but without it, life is not worth living… you have got to give them hope". The Star represents hope shining through the darkness. It symbolizes courage and faith in the future. No one exemplifies this hope for Queer people better than Harvey Milk.

THE STAR

THE MOON

When you find the right path to be on, whether it be for self, home, love, or career, this is no guarantee of success or great accomplishment. Although finding your true calling is one of life's greatest goals, it is often only the beginning of a new series of neuroses. The Moon is the harbinger of these particular emotions, often manifested as self-deception, self-sabotage and loss of dignity. The last thing you want to do once you've finally found your way is to once again become lost, but The Moon is a will-o-the-wisp that beckons you to stray, or terrifies you enough that you turn back in utter fright. Although The Moon shines a light on all the horrors around you, all it illuminates are the illusions, uncertainties, and doubts you have about yourself and your abilities. But The Moon truly has no light of its own (it is the Unconscious); it is only the evening reflection off of a dormant and temporarily subdued Sun. When The Moon appears in a spread, you must confront your anxieties, the darkest lies you've told yourself, and the ones you've told others. Look to the cards around it for guidance, and also for where in your life The Moon is going to attempt to obscure you and keep you in its stead.

The Moon also has the ability to paralyze and create stagnation. You can find yourself standing still, making no progress, convincing yourself that how far you've come is the best you can do, the best you're meant to do, for The Moon will have you second guess everything.

The Moon often manifests as other people. Those who project their fears onto others, who use repression and moral panic to control them, are often people who have been utterly conquered by The Moon, who forever linger in the dark, themselves having become the vampires, wolves and beasts who pace just off the path, just inside the trees, ready to grab anyone who wanders too close.

The Moon is ruled by the sign of Pisces, so it's a card of Water, being its least malignant when near Cups or other Water-based Major Arcana. The Moon has the least power over love and matters of the heart, for in such situations there is another person (the loved one) to guide you through the mire. Its presence should still be heeded, of course, for paranoid uncertainty is still a threat wherever it lies in a spread. When near many Earth-based cards, beware of drug abuse and false senses of security or vulnerability. When near many Air-based cards, The Moon can, in extreme cases, cause madness or hysteria, but in milder ones bring about prophetic dreams and nightmares. The most dangerous position is when surrounded by Fire-based cards, as The Moon heralds emotional illness, spiritual death, a life without empathy, forever wandering blind through The Abyss.

Tennessee Williams (1911-1983) American playwright and poet in the Southern Gothic tradition.

Williams was a sickly and frail child who was a disappointment to his overbearing, alcoholic father. He was always close to his sister, Rose, who suffered from schizophrenia and was institutionalized following a prefrontal lobotomy ordered by her parents.

Throughout all this, his mother maintained the veneer of southern gentility. Later, Williams' own life was to be characterized by alcoholism, amphetamine addiction, depression, and fear of mental illness.

Tennessee Williams' hugely successful plays – *The Glass Menagerie, A Streetcar Named Desire, Cat on a Hot Tin Roof, Suddenly Last Summer* - are pitched emotional dramas filled with madness, addiction, denial and sexual repression. Many were made into movies and were among the most successful box office hits of the 1950s and 1960s. He tapped into the concealed dysfunction of American family life and exposed the shadow side: fear, anxiety, and emotionally crippling dynamics at work.

The Moon card represents this neurotic and self-limiting side of the human soul. The Moon casts shadows that contain our emotional baggage. Few people have understood the motivating power of our unconscious fears as well as Tennessee Williams. He and his most famous creation, Blanche Dubois, in many ways his shadow-self, are The Moon.

THE MOON

THE SUN

Although the appearance of this card can mean the emergence from darkness into 'the light', The Sun most definitely signifies expansion, achievement, happiness and unabashed pleasure and glory. Nowhere in the Tarot is one card's definition as opposite as the card preceding it as is the case with The Sun and The Moon. Following 'the dark night of the soul' revealed in The Moon, The Sun exemplifies success, revitalization, and freedom from recent situations or circumstances which were holding you back, keeping you fearful or causing neurotic, paranoiac reactions to your environment and those in it.

Perhaps you no longer care what others think in regard to your beliefs, morality, sexuality, or spirituality. Or maybe the fear of death is conquered, the fear of failure, the fear of loneliness – these conquests can change your life in ways so potent it can truly feel like the sun is shining for the first time. As with all other cards, look for where The Sun appears in the spread to reach its full understanding.

Another manifestation of The Sun is the realization that what you call 'contentment' is actually a strong manifestation of love. Or rather, that they are one and the same; contentment is an avatar of love. This can shine upon relationships, careers, environments, the partner, ideas, and dreams – and when it does, you should accept it as a moment of truth. There is a great falsehood peddled that love always needs to be worked on. This isn't always so. Sometimes love just 'is' – this is The Sun. It connotes so many of the great, positive things in life, already affirmed earlier, but ultimately, it is the card of this revealed truth-love in the state of contentment.

The Sun card is ruled by the Sun itself, so it's a card of Fire, being of greatest benefit when near Wands or other Fire-based Major Arcana. Few cards can match The Sun's intrinsic spirituality, and if near many Fire-based cards The Sun is an awakening of the highest sort, a discovery of supreme pleasure, enlightenment (perhaps our true love, or our relationship to a Godhead), and therefore freedom. When near Earth-based cards, The Sun signifies either material riches and gain, or the reaching of optimal health, vitality and physical well-being. With Air-based cards, The Sun warrants intellectual breakthroughs, the manifestations of these discoveries, and helps nullify the coldness of many Swords. However, when near too many Cups and Water-based cards, The Sun's light can become dimmed, reflected and false, bringing egotism, narcissism, and ultimately a straying from the path.

Jane Addams (1860 – 1935) Social reformer and pacifist.

One of the big social justice initiatives of the late nineteenth century was the Settlement Movement, where middle-class volunteers provided education and shared social activities for the poor. Jane Addams established the US's most successful Settlement House in Chicago in 1889. Functioning on three ethical principles – teaching by example, practicing cooperation, and egalitarian social relations – it became a center for social reform activity. Jane Addams is often attributed with introducing social reform and justice as core principles of modern Social Work. She and her life partner, Mary Smith, lived together for forty years. Mary used her wealth to support Jane's work.

Addams was also a world-famous peace activist. She was president of the Women's International League for Peace and Freedom and was an early advocate of the link between peace and social justice. She was highly critical of the military practice of giving soldiers alcohol and drugs before they charged from the trenches across no man's land. She was awarded the Nobel Peace Prize in 1931.

Jane Addams was a shining example of how to live openly and without fear. She is The Sun demonstrating expansion, achievement, happiness, unabashed pleasure and glory.

XIX

THE SUN

JUDGMENT

You make decisions or come to conclusions that, in the moment, might seem unimportant or only slightly significant, but time eventually shows that they initiated distinct and unambiguous steps in our lives, leading us to great awareness. When this card appears in a spread, you should pay closer attention than to almost any other card in the entire deck. Its presence signifies that the question at hand in the current layout is of definitive and monumental spiritual significance, one that should not be underestimated. Be aware that the concerns of the spread are actually life-changing decisions, often when you don't realize or didn't suspect. It means the end of an old current in your life, the closing of an entire matter, the end of a way of being, an epiphany and also an opening up to endless new possibilities and entirely new states. Past manifestations of this card as representing The Last Judgment and the death/rebirth of a Phoenix are accurate in their vertical, transcendent, ascending degrees and traits, if not ultimately limiting in breadth to Judgment's certain, strong relationship with an 'awakening' that can also be mental, emotional and material, and not just spiritual. Jung's synchronicity lives in this card.

The more other Major Arcana or Aces there are in the rest of the spread, the more drastic and intense the destruction of old ways will be, and the more momentous the change in your life. However, the appearance of Judgment at its least forceful will still bring about some kind of change in, for example, your position in a particular situation, job or relationship. If near Court Cards, it can signify that others are becoming aware of your powers, your abilities, and your ways of being, and are themselves making big changes in their own lives in order to accommodate you or lift you up to a higher state, either romantically, through work (as in promotion), or even via the beginning of a new friendship. Judgment in its plainest, weakest, albeit still positive manifestation signifies an understanding of a matter that was previously confusing, or a simple, easy letting go of unnecessary or lingering memories.

Judgment is ruled by the element of Fire, being of greatest intensity and influence when near Wands or other Fire-based Major Arcana. Judgment surrounded by Fire truly is a Phoenix, bringing rebirth in a most intense, positive, and public manifestation. If near much Earth, Judgment can mean a respite from physical and material trials, or a purging of materiality. Surrounded by Air, Judgment becomes a period of great contemplation and appraisal, perhaps granting a long lead-up to whatever decision it ultimately forces upon you. However, if near too much Water, Judgment can fall apart, resulting in inertia, the continued belief in things no longer true, the inability to see clearly, missed opportunities, and/or a complete loss of momentum.

James Baldwin (1924 – 1987) American essayist, novelist, playwright and critic.

Few people have understood and articulated the legacy of racism in the United States, as well as James Baldwin. Born into poverty in Harlem, he embraced Pentecostalism early but soon rejected it for the isolated life of the writer. He was active in the civil rights movement and was a committed Socialist throughout his life. He lived most of his adult life in self-imposed exile in France.

Baldwin never settled for easy answers. He understood that racism, past and present, is not something we can easily put to rest. "I'm not interested in anybody's guilt. Guilt is a luxury that we can no longer afford. I know you didn't do it, and I didn't do it either, but I am responsible for it because I am a man and a citizen of this country, and you are responsible for it, for the very same reason". His novel, *Giovanni's Room*, was one of the first to detail the awakening of homosexuality in an adult man and its sometimes messy consequences.

Judgment's epiphany requires a coming to terms with the past in order to move forward. It requires maturity and experience. Baldwin brings Judgment to bear on the post-war America of the 1950s and '60s and coldly exposes its past – not as an act of revenge but as an act of love. As he said, "I love America more than any other country in the world and, exactly for this reason, I insist on the right to criticize her". We may never see a more discerning judge than James Baldwin.

JUDGMENT

43

THE UNIVERSE

Unlike the move from The Moon to The Sun, the one from Judgment to The Universe couldn't be more complimentary. The decision taken in Judgment leads to a wholly positive amalgamation represented by The Universe. The card signifies the definite, positive ending of a chapter in your life, and the deep breath before leaping into the next great unknown. Whatever the true answer to the question at hand is becomes absolutely clear under The Universe's influence – a crystallization of the reason for the matter that had been troubling you. This manifests as what you thought you were inquiring about actually leading to an entirely new revelation, and of greater importance than ever realized – the interconnectedness between all of your complexes. The Universe brings a feeling of intense clarity and insight, and rewards being patient and persevering. It also rewards the achievement of having synthesized knowledge and experience, tension and anxiety into an expansive and benevolent new view of yourself and the world.

You've so successfully navigated what was disturbing and blocking you that you now stand above it, showing mastery over it. This is fulfillment in its greatest form, for it is equally spiritual, emotional, mental, and material. The answer to most 'self' questions ultimately lies in learning what you honestly want from life, and The Universe grants you an understanding of your true place within the system or world you occupy. At last, you learn that this must be a place of love, and that the greatest, truest joy comes from accepting your mortality, and giving back to the world what you've learned on your journey. But this chapter of steadiness and symmetry, too, must end. Here, you turn the page. Another Fool lies before you, although now you are better-equipped thanks to The Universe's assurance of your having grown.

The Universe is ruled by Saturn, which in turn rules Capricorn, an Earth sign. The Universe indicates knowledge you already possess from previous experience, and when it appears, it is calling upon you to summon up something known within to help solve the current problem. Look to what surrounds it, what is near it - it is likely in what these cards represent that the answers will be found. More than most cards, The Universe is a signifier. If too much Air surrounds The Universe, this can mean reaching far beyond your limits, not doing the work that's truly needed, being caught up in vacant worldliness, losing energy right before completion, and/or unhappy endings that happen for no reason whatsoever.

Michel Foucault (1926 – 1984): French philosopher and activist who changed the way we think about bodies, sex, and power.

During the 1960s and '70s, Foucault was one of the Continental philosophers who turned the academic world on its head by challenging the basis of traditional power structures. He explored the relationship between power and knowledge and showed how they both serve to channel our thinking and control our behavior. Critical of traditional biological explanations of 'fringe' behaviors such as sexuality, madness, and criminality, he argued that power and discipline limit the ways in which we think about ourselves and our identities.

Foucault pointed out that same-sex activity had, in the past, existed as behavior, usually deviant behavior; but only more recently had it become a subjectivity or an identity, rendering the person deviant rather than the behavior itself. Foucault does not view this development as purely negative – homosexual subjectivity/identity has given us a rich queer culture.

A regular visitor to gay saunas and S&M sex clubs, Foucault lived by his own unconventional truths. He died of AIDS in 1984. In the decades since, Foucault has had a huge influence on Feminist and Queer theorists. In 2007 he was named as the most cited scholar in the humanities.

In many ways he marks the positive ending of an old chapter in human thought and represents the deep breath before leaping into the next great unknown: "There are times in life when the question of knowing if one can think differently than one thinks, and perceive differently than one sees, is absolutely necessary if one is to go on looking and reflecting at all." He is The Universe incarnate.

THE UNIVERSE

THE MINOR ARCANA

ACE OF WANDS

Strength, ingenuity, and audacity. An eruption of energy bursting from and through instituted, static oppression. To substitute petrification and fear with courage and inventiveness. The crown of creation. Determination, natural force, and iconoclasm.

Ill-dignified: To burn too hard, too fast. A lack of understanding. Disfunction. To be in too much of a rush, and/or to become weighed down by tyrannies. Perpetual frustrations.

Radclyffe Hall (1880 – 1943) Lesbian English poet and writer who created the first 'sapphic' novel.

Although she wrote many accomplished novels and books of poetry, Radclyffe Hall will be forever remembered as the author of *The Well of Loneliness*. The novel depicts the social isolation and rejection experienced by LGBT people and shows how this damages not just individuals but society as a whole. Hall's goals in writing the book were explicitly political; she aimed to break the silence and end the taboo around the subject of homosexuality. Refusing her publisher's permission to edit, she said, "I have put my pen at the service of some of the most persecuted and misunderstood people in the world. So far as I know nothing of the kind has ever been attempted before in fiction."

Despite early attempts to ban the book – or perhaps because of its notoriety – *The Well of Loneliness* became an early source of information for generations of young queers.

Radclyffe Hall is the Ace of Wands, courageously smashing old perceptions and ushering in a fresh understanding. An iconoclast who created one of the earliest ways of seeing ourselves.

ACE OF WANDS

TWO OF WANDS

Authority, invocation, audacity. A creative idea willed into being after much decision, discovery and achievement. To substitute doubt and delays with boldness and initiation. The seed of innovation. Recognition of one's own wisdom, and to move forward with accomplishing your goals with said wisdom. To take a leadership position while still extolling the virtues of partnership.

Ill-dignified: Impatience, stubbornness, and disorder. To willfully ignore or downplay what you don't have knowledge of so as not to have to reassess your beliefs. Fear of failure disguised as apathy.

John Cage (1912 – 1992) Gay American avant-garde composer and music theorist.

John Cage's music is a core part of the twentieth-century avant-garde. Through non-standard use of musical instruments Cage sought to undermine our fixed notions of what music is. He questioned our assumed definitions and undertook a theoretical exploration of the aesthetics of performance. His piece, *4'33''*, is performed by a group of musicians who sit with their instruments for that time as the audience focuses on the ambient noise.

He sometimes referred to himself as an inventor rather than a composer and famously developed the prepared piano, where everyday objects are lodged between the strings to alter the timbre of the notes. Cage also incorporated chance into his work; this grew from an interest in Eastern thinking, especially the I Ching: *Imaginary Landscape No. 4* uses 24 performers 'playing' 12 radios. He also collaborated with his life partner, **Merce Cunningham (1919 – 2009)** on dance pieces incorporating chance elements.

Cunningham was himself a leading light within the avant-garde and is regarded as one of the masters of modern dance.

Audacity, creativity, and bold innovation in partnership with others characterize both John Cage and Merce Cunningham as the Two of Wands.

TWO OF WANDS

THREE OF WANDS

Integrity, vigor and magnetism. A new and exciting endeavor that will have much success as long as your self-confidence doesn't turn into pride. To substitute struggle and irrational fears with concentrated efforts and new resourceful friendships. The house of foresight and growth. Being of noble character, full of capabilities, and having made the best-laid plans.

Ill-dignified: Smugness, arrogance and procrastination. To have charged full steam ahead against obstacles without having made any plan(s), often due to conceit alone. A long-term goal never accomplished.

Jose Sarría (1923 – 2013) Legendary gay activist, drag queen, and founder of the Imperial Court System.

A native of San Francisco, Jose Sarría led a colorful early life, which included being barred from teaching after being convicted of soliciting. Following military service Sarría began his career as a drag performer in the North Beach bohemian Black Cat club.

Known as the Nightingale of Montgomery Street he also found his activist voice by opposing police harassment of the city's gay community. In 1961, Sarría ran for the San Francisco Board of Supervisors becoming the first openly gay candidate for political office in the U.S. His 6,000 votes forced the political establishment to recognize the power of the 'gay vote'.

In 1965, he created the persona of the Widow Norton and established the Imperial Court system. Since then, the Court has grown into an international association of charitable organizations raising millions of dollars through their drag-themed fundraisers.

Jose Sarría and the Imperial Court, with their vigor, resourcefulness and self-confidence, are the Three of Wands. Their noble character raises them above adversity into something truly magnificent and humanist.

THREE OF WANDS

FOUR OF WANDS

Achievements, principles, and harmonies. A cheerful celebration following a virtuous and successful struggle, often against the dominion of an institution or persons of authority. To substitute coarseness and uselessness with refinement and cleverness. The pillar of support. Perfection, beginnings, the synthesis of independence and community.

Ill-dignified: Restlessness, miscommunications, and/or a fear of commitment. To be in too much of a hurry and to choose to hear what you want to hear. A besotted transition.

Christine Jorgensen (1926 – 1989) American trans woman activist, actress, singer and a pioneer recipient of sexual reassignment surgery.

Often credited as the first person to have SRS, Christine Jorgensen was the first case in which hormone treatments and surgery were successfully combined. Following her transition in 1951, she spoke frankly and articulately about her gender identity before the surgery and the sense of completeness and happiness that followed. The best-known trans person in the US in the 1950s, '60s, and '70s, she appeared on many TV shows and was the subject of dozens of magazine articles. Articulate, intelligent and witty, Jorgensen charmed her interviewers and helped kick off the discussion that would undermine the notion of gender as a fixed binary.

Christine Jorgensen also had minor success as an actress and singer. However, she was prohibited from marrying her fiancée because her birth certificate identified her as male.

Christine, as the Four of Wands, struggled against authority and convention to achieve a happy conclusion. Her transition replaced personal discord with inner harmony and produced a more perfect version of herself.

FOUR OF WANDS

FIVE OF WANDS

Arguments, cravings, and challenges. A struggle in which you long not for victory but for harmony and agreement, for the elimination of tension and anxiety. To substitute achievement and elegance for a chance at greater glory, but to end up with dissent and brutality. The gateway to violence. Spitefulness and volcanic tempers; however, these are the fires from which the phoenix rises.

Ill-dignified: Deflection, a narrow miss, and/or the avoidance of conflict. To settle for less than you deserve, thus laying the groundwork for a possible future conflict. The need to increase your focus.

The Cockettes (1969 – 1972) Queer, anarchic, avant-garde, hippie performance troupe.

The Cockettes were born from the hippie maelstrom of late 1960s San Francisco. Their psychedelic, gender-bending, and chaotic performances used drag, Old Hollywood themes and eclectic accoutrements to captivate and entertain West Coast audiences. Their original productions included *Tinsel Tarts in a Hot Coma, Journey to the Center of Uranus*, *Pearls Over Shanghai* and the underground movie *Tricia's Wedding,* which parodied the presidential daughter's actual marriage ceremony.

In 1971, the Cockettes were invited to bring their transgressive, guerrilla theater to New York City and perform in front of the world's media. This caused a philosophical split within the troupe. Some wanted to continue with the free, LSD-infused, anarchic performances, while others advocated a more structured, and commercially-oriented approach. The Cockettes bombed in New York, and they split after much infighting and acrimony.

Sadly, their struggle between integrity and achievement with the ensuing dissent, argument and grudges makes The Cockettes the Five of Wands.

FIVE OF WANDS

SIX OF WANDS

Creative success, masterful control, and artistic or spiritual gains. A personal reinvention or triumph (likely brought about by cleverness and inspiration) after a period of strife, imbalance, or uncertainty. To substitute tension and conflict with self-sufficiency and appreciation of others. The bridge between strength and love. The shedding of old skins and ways of being/believing, acknowledgement of contributions and creations, and the adoration that comes with it.

Ill-dignified: Arrogance, rudeness, 'your way or the highway'. To cover up a lack of confidence or surety with extroverted and/or disreputable behavior. Over-adornment.

Freddie Mercury (1946 – 1991) Gay British singer, songwriter and flamboyant front-man for the rock band Queen.

Farrokh Bulsara was born in Zanzibar. The son of an Indian civil servant in the British Colonial Office, he was educated in a boarding school. In 1970 he became Freddie Mercury and named his band Queen over the objection of the record label. Queen were quite simply one of the biggest rock bands of all time – 18 number-one albums, 18 number-one singles and record sales of over 300 million. Their songs ranged from crusading anthems, "We Will Rock You" through heartbreak, "Somebody to Love" to the sublime fantasy of "Bohemian Rhapsody".

It wasn't just the music that made Queen great – it was also Freddie's persona. His clothes, performance, flamboyant strut, and soaring voice all combined to make him one of the most beloved pop artists of his time, and still so today. But he was also intensely private. After years denying he had AIDS, a visibly ill Freddie died of the disease in 1991.

Artistically masterful, Farrokh triumphantly reinvented himself as Freddie. As the Six of Wands, he urged us to be strong while remaining open to love.

SIX OF WANDS

SEVEN OF WANDS

Perseverance, valor, and willingness to take on challenges. Finding the strength, often at the last minute, to nobly fight for your belief or position, and having the spirit to cope with what is likely a losing battle. To lose progress and status due to defending your arguments and trying to hold your ground. The wheel of conflict. Coming to the realization that there is an inherent compromise in all forms of struggle, to accept setbacks and defeats, and yet to never lose your faith in the cause, whatever it may be.

Ill-dignified: Feeling overwhelmed and/or hopeless. Backing down from an argument. To be emotional when it's the last thing that will help. Guilt for being unprepared and taking on too much.

Leonard Matlovich (1943 – 1988) Vietnam War veteran, Purple Heart and Bronze Star recipient who outed himself in the U.S. military.

Leonard Matlovich was decorated for his service in Vietnam. Injured on his third tour of duty, he later became an instructor in Air Force race relations. With a clean military record, Leonard Matlovich chose to out himself to challenge the military's ban on homosexuals. He was quickly given a less-than-honorable discharge after refusing to sign a declaration that he would never again 'practice' homosexuality. Working with activist Frank Kameny, he sued the US Air Force for wrongful dismissal. The case became a media sensation and Leonard appeared on TV and magazine covers. He was the public face of the struggle for gays in the military.

Matlovich's challenge ultimately failed, and he was awarded a small cash settlement. He died of AIDS. His tombstone, a memorial to all gay veterans, reads 'When I was in the military, they gave me a medal for killing two men and a discharge for loving one'. It wasn't until 2011 that military gays, lesbians, and bisexuals were protected. And the ban on Trans personnel wasn't lifted until 2021.

Leonard Matlovich fought against injustice, even knowing the odds were against him. Like the Seven of Wands, he persevered and kept his faith in the cause.

SEVEN OF WANDS

EIGHT OF WANDS

Confidence in action, boldness of speech, freedom in all manners and directions. Harnessing energies and exploiting events so as to bring about a change in the way that others perceive or understand you or what you represent. To swiftly move from compromise or defeat to sudden anger. Finding the finish line closer than previously foreseen, or aspects of life moving more quickly than you're comfortable with. An upcoming event, journey, or message that will transform forever your beliefs and/or your sense of self.

Ill-dignified: An opportunity missed or squandered due to too much force applied too soon and/or too strongly. A long delay of something which should've come much sooner. Something that was over much too soon.

Compton's Cafeteria Rioters (1966) Transgender and sex worker riot against police harassment.

Compton's Cafeteria in San Francisco's Tenderloin was a hang-out for the city's transgender community who were often unwelcome even in gay and lesbian bars. The police liked to aggravate Compton's trans customers in response to calls from disgruntled Cafeteria staff. In August 1966 (three years before Stonewall), police were called and started to hassle as usual. However, one transwoman had had enough and fought back. So started the riot that resulted in destroyed furniture and smashed windows. The Cafeteria was picketed on the following evenings and police were again called to handle the situation. The riots continued over several nights.

The riots were one of the earliest instances of trans people fighting back against discrimination and brutality. As a direct result the National Transsexual Counselling Unit was established to provide peer-to-peer counselling, support, and advocacy. It also led to a reduction in police harassment of trans community members in San Francisco.

The sudden burst of righteous anger at Compton's Cafeteria brought real change. The Eight of Wands is about transforming the status quo with a confident, energetic jolt.

EIGHT OF WANDS

NINE OF WANDS

Strength, resilience, and the honorable use of power. Having the courage and personal resources to stand up against all odds and succeed at every turn; or the wisdom and spirit to resist all tests, temptations and enemies that come your way. To realize that true stability means knowing when to change, and that losing your fear of change is the best means to maintain stability. Not having any trepidation or worry about an issue, but nonetheless to stay on guard and take precautions to keep your position. Defense as the best offense.

Ill-dignified: Being overly defensive, tense and/or anxious. To be paranoid about losing it all at any moment. Being dogged by bad health. In the worst significations, it can mean megalomania and despotism.

Barbara Gittings (1932 – 2007) Lesbian American LGBT rights activist and leader.

Barbara Gittings' lifelong ambition was to tear away the shroud of invisibility covering queer experience. She tackled this on many fronts, becoming one of the most engaged and effective gay activists of her time. In 1965, during the very early days of gay liberation, Gittings was among a small number of visible activists. She edited *The Ladder*, the magazine for The Daughters of Bilitis (the first lesbian civil rights organization in the U.S.) and was part of the group that Brenda Howard (Three of Cups) organized for the first Stonewall commemoration that grew into Gay Pride. She was a leader, along with Richard Isay (Four of Swords), in the movement to have homosexuality declassified as a mental disorder.

Her most enduring legacy is likely to be her work with the Gay Task Force of the American Library Association, advocating for the inclusion of gay-positive materials in libraries throughout the country. She knew that this was the first place many young people went for information.

Courageously standing up for our rights and succeeding against the odds, Barbara Gittings is the Nine of Wands. She fearlessly led and created real change.

NINE OF WANDS

Domination, cruelty and totalitarianism. Spiritually destructive, and guilt-ridden by your own formidable strength and power. Selfish, malicious and slanderous actions coming back to haunt you, or you yourself are the victim of such forces that are set upon you by another. This card is the element of fire without any other elemental balance, as far removed as possible from the divine, void of heart, mind or body, all-engulfing and all-purifying. This is oppression. This is fascism. This is the selling of the soul. The Ten of Wands will violently explode and eventually burn itself up in the process, like a supernova, a phoenix, or a tyrant. However, the ground for a new seed, a new Ace of Wands is prepared.

Ill-dignified: Making up excuses and reasons for avoiding life and love. Believing life and love to be the great oppressors. Having to make do with where your own beliefs have got you.

Ernst Röhm (1887 – 1934) Gay German military officer and an early leading member of the Nazi party.

Ernst Röhm was a political ally and close friend of Adolf Hitler. As head of the Nazi SA stormtroopers, 'the brownshirts', he attacked and intimidated anyone opposing the Nazi viewpoint. The brownshirts were at the center of the Nazi coup of 1933 when power was seized from the German government. Röhm was openly homosexual, as were many of the SA leaders. In 1931, a German newspaper published his letters discussing his sex life. He saw no conflict between his sexuality and his Fascist beliefs.

By 1934, senior Nazi party members considered the SA too powerful, so they fabricated evidence and plotted to destroy Röhm. Hitler summoned the SA leadership to Munich and on June 30, 'the Night of the Long Knives', had most of them executed.

Röhm himself was imprisoned and offered the option to commit suicide. He refused and was subsequently executed point blank.

Ernst Röhm's totalitarianism and brutality ultimately led to his own destruction. Like the Ten of Wands, he was the center of violent events that eventually imploded and purged him of his power and dominance.

TEN OF WANDS

PRINCESS OF WANDS

This card's appearance in a reading heralds a state of great energy and yearning for something better. It's time for you to seek out new experiences, to be bold and audacious, and not to let anyone stand in the way of your passions and objectives. This is the moment to *do it*, so don't miss your chance. Be brazen and adventurous. Though your actions may seem excessive to a few others, don't let that stop you.

Ill-dignified: If surrounded by too many Cups and/or Water-based Major Arcana, this card is a warning against shallowness, melodrama, lying, volatility and dangerous sexual situations.

Tallulah Bankhead (1902-1968) Bisexual American actress famous for her larger-than-life personality.

Born into an Alabama political dynasty, Tallulah rejected her conservative upbringing in favor of a life on the stage and screen. Bankhead was quite unabashed. She lived large and wasn't afraid to talk about it – her quotes are as infamous as her life. Among them: "Let's not quibble! I'm the foe of moderation, the champion of excess," "I'm as pure as the driven slush," and the queer-embracing "My father warned me about men and booze, but he never mentioned a word about women and cocaine". She described herself as 'ambisextrous' and was rumored to have had affairs with many famous women of the time.

She could, however, also be reckless. In 1933, Tallulah almost died following an emergency hysterectomy resulting from an untreated STD. Earlier in the 1920s, she was investigated by Britain's MI5 for seducing Eton schoolboys and encouraging 'indecent and unnatural acts.'

Tallulah exemplifies the Princess of Wands through her audacious and shameless flaunting of convention and search for novelty. She lived fully and loved to shock.

PRINCESS OF WANDS

PRINCE OF WANDS

This card's appearance in a reading announces an environment of fortitude, leadership, quick action, and innovation. You will either find yourself approaching a challenging situation that you should charge into, or you will meet someone of younger spirit, mind or age who is creatively inspirational, impetuous, artistically strong and bold of heart and will inspire you into action. Regardless, ride this wave of enthusiasm, lucidity and forward-thinking.

Ill-dignified: If surrounded by too many Cups and/or Water-based Major Arcana, this card is a warning against irritation, self-doubt, and taking on too much. Also, cruel, intolerant, and narcissistic people are particularly present during this time.

Rainer Werner Fassbinder (1945-1982) Exceedingly prolific gay German filmmaker.

Although born into a solidly bourgeois family, Fassbinder became a sharp observer of middle-class hypocrisy and the way people, particularly women, were forced to navigate it. He had lovers of both sexes, but mainly men, with whom he often became explosively, violently tangled.

He achieved international recognition in the mid-seventies with many films, including *Ali: Fear Eats the Soul*, and *Fox and His Friends*. This meant larger budgets and international exposure for his later films, most famously the *BRD Trilogy*, and the 15-hour epic, *Berlin Alexanderplatz*. Fassbinder's volcanic creative energy and charismatic personality were a central feature in West Germany's post-war self-examination.

His personal life was often chaotic and fueled by drugs to support this maddening productivity. He sacrificed anything and everything for the end vision - so it's easy to see why the cruelty inherent in everyday relationships is a recurring theme in Fassbinder's work.

Fassbinder exemplifies the Prince of Wands by the sheer force of his creativity. Impetuous, courageous, and spirited, he led a group of artists to produce a body of work that challenged a nation.

PRINCE OF WANDS

QUEEN OF WANDS

This card's appearance in a reading announces a time to be alert, hard-working, and persistent, but also sympathetic and open to flexibility. You will realize that you need to be a person of independent beliefs, actions and/or means, and to remain tough and aloof, or, you will meet someone of older heart, mind or age who is spirited, graceful, and with kismet-like attractive powers. They are full of inspiration and wisdom, and you should heed their advice, or learn from their focused example. Nevertheless, this card heralds endurance, willpower, generosity, and recognizing your own spiritual truths.

Ill-dignified: If surrounded by too many Cups or Water-based Major Arcana, this card is a warning against stubbornness, authoritarianism, and/or infidelity being directed towards you by another.

Marlene Dietrich (1901-1992) Bisexual German-born actress and singer whose astonishing and inimitable career spanned most of the twentieth century.

Her earliest professional incarnation was that of a chorus girl in Berlin revues and vaudeville. Eventually, she was 'discovered' by Josef von Sternberg, who cast her as Lola Lola in *The Blue Angel*, her most enduring role. She moved to Hollywood and quickly became a huge hit, often playing sexy, strong women in harsh, masculine settings. During this time Dietrich also developed a successful recording career using her husky contralto voice to infuse the songs with sensitivity and subdued drama.

Dietrich transitioned her movie career into a successful cabaret act in which she performed the first half wearing sheer, body-hugging dresses only to sing her way through the second half in top hat and tails, making her one of the originators of modern gender-bending. Dietrich also had many affairs with men and women, often overlapping; she confidently embraced her sexuality and oozed cool.

Marlene, a German on the side of the Allies, was a resilient and determined woman motivated by her beliefs. She exemplifies the Queen of Wands' strength and independent thinking.

QUEEN OF WANDS

KING OF WANDS

This card's appearance in a reading indicates a time to recognize the traits of authority, determination and creative vitality within yourself, and to be an advocate for your beliefs for which you are now very certain. You've been held up to scrutiny, and passed the tests, so now is the time to implement with dignity and assurance. But this is also a time of confident deliberation, as you want to leave no room for error or criticism. If you remember to protect what you believe in, to stay ardent to your principles, and to remain honest throughout, nothing can stop you.

Ill-dignified: If surrounded by too many Cups or Water-based Major Arcana, this card is a warning against moral superiority and/or brutality, perhaps even of a vindictive nature, affecting your life.

Gore Vidal (1925 – 2012) Queer American patrician, political commentator, and writer; one of the great iconoclasts, polemicists, and wits of his time.

Gore Vidal was born into the heart of the American establishment. Throughout his life he maintained this privileged social position while challenging many of its core beliefs.

Vidal's novels address homosexuality (*The City and the Pillar*), gender norms (*Myra Breckenridge*) and political corruption (*Washington D.C.*). His essays run the gamut of U.S. liberal-progressive political issues. Highly critical of George W. Bush's presidency, Gore Vidal wrote about the Iraq War, the Patriot Act and government involvement in the 9/11 attacks. Sometimes imperious, his views have brought him into public conflict with many other cultural critics.

One of Vidal's more controversial opinions concerns the nature of sexuality. He rejects the labels homo, hetero and bi believing instead that we are all pansexual and respond to the societal norms which vary over time. He ascribed the longevity of his relationship with his life partner to the fact that they never had sex.

Gore Vidal's strong sense of authority and determination make him a confident and outspoken critic of modern culture. Like the King of Wands, he stuck to his guns and consequently was unstoppable.

KING OF WANDS

ACE OF CUPS

Fruitfulness, elation and self-realization. Excess from satiety flows into a new, remarkable and singular purity. To substitute anger and resentment with joy and peace. The crown of love. Intensity, a wanted overwhelmingness, and surprising success.

Ill-dignified: Emotional proxies, restriction to a particular reaction, and/or holding back your true feelings. To become drowned in a single, over-expressed emotion. Preposterously thin-skinned.

Ma Rainey (1886 – 1939) Lesbian African-American Blues singer and recording artist who is considered the Mother of the Blues.

Ma Rainey started performing in her early teens. By 1914, she was a well-established minstrel and vaudeville show star, eventually making her first recordings in 1923; she went on to record over 100 records, which brought her national fame. Ma Rainey had a powerful voice and developed a 'moaning' style of singing. Unfortunately, the quality of her vinyl recordings is generally poor and fails to convey the full majesty of her voice. She is widely regarded as one of the originators of Blues music and in 1990 was inducted into the Rock and Roll Hall of Fame.

Rainey's songs sometimes made reference to her lesbianism, especially *Prove It on Me,* which was a response to her arrest for taking part in an orgy in her home with her female backing singers.

One might argue that the Blues is the art form that most effectively transforms anger and resentment into joy and peace. Ma Rainey is the Ace of Cups, being a strong queer voice at the birth of the Blues. Her emotional intensity, vocal intuition and personal openness are the seeds of love.

ACE OF CUPS

77

Attraction, emotional harmony, and alliances. The start of an intense friendship, physical relationship, or partnership within an established community. To substitute repression and exhaustion with pleasure and togetherness. The seed of love. Unification between what you are and what you need. To submit to and share your love with the world, and to fully accept the joy this brings.

Ill-dignified: Debauchery, wastefulness and friction. To be in a loving, yet completely imbalanced relationship, often due to an imposition of will. The exclusion of all others for the sake of the one.

Gertrude Stein (1874 – 1946) Lesbian American modernist art collector, novelist, playwright and poet.

Although raised in Oakland, California, by 1903 Gertrude Stein based herself in Paris and came into contact with many of the greatest artists of her generation. She was a prolific modernist who used stream-of-consciousness as a literary response to abstraction in painting. Gertrude bought works by painters, many of whom were to become the major artists of the 20th-century. Much of Gertrude Stein's writing is either experimental or documentary. A multiplicitous, heterodox, contradictory and frustrating thinker, Stein espoused reactionary, progressive, pro-fascist, anti-patriarchal, pro-immigration, and pro-Democratic views at various and sometimes the same times throughout her life.

However, she is best known for *The Autobiography of Alice B. Toklas*. Named for her life partner **Alice B. Toklas (1877 – 1967),** whom she met in 1907, the book is in fact Gertrude's own autobiography. Alice later published *The Alice B. Toklas Cookbook* containing a recipe for pot brownies. Gertrude and Alice were devoted to each other and wrote hundreds of intimate letters. They built their lives around each other and became each other's support.

Gertrude and Alice lived a life of emotional harmony, love, partnership and togetherness, which typify the Two of Cups. A love accepted and shared that found beauty despite the troubled times in which they lived.

TWO OF CUPS

THREE OF CUPS

Abundance, bonding, and generosity. A coming together between strangers, friends, or members of a community for a common, benevolent goal. To substitute wanton foolishness and waste with sensual joy and bounty. The house of humanity and inspiration. To recognize the emotional needs of others, but also to accept their transience.

Ill-dignified: Remoteness, emptiness, and the refusal of help. To have one's emotions silenced due to their perceived pointlessness, or due to jealousy. An unrequited love, or friendship lost.

Brenda Howard (1946 – 2005) Trailblazing American feminist and bisexual LGBT rights activist who is considered the Mother of Pride.

During the late 1960s, Brenda Howard was active in the anti-war and feminist movements. However, it was 1969's Stonewall Riots (Fortune) that crystalized her activism around the gay liberation movement. Coordinating with others to commemorate the first anniversary of the riots, Howard conceived of a weeklong festival celebrating queer identity. This was the genesis of Gay Pride, now celebrated the world over by millions of LGBT people and their allies. Howard was also instrumental in organizing the 1994 *March on Washington for Lesbian, Gay and Bi Equal Rights and Liberation.*

Today, there are hundreds of LGBT Pride events around the world. With a mixture of parades, carnivál and serious political messages, Pride has become one of the most visible manifestations of the LGBT community. For many straight people as well, this is their opportunity to voice their support for queerness and sexual diversity.

With their joyful embrace of community, Brenda Howard and Pride are the Three of Cups. The abundant celebration of difference and simple love that is Pride continue to bring us all closer together.

THREE OF CUPS

FOUR OF CUPS

Extravagance, fragility, and taking life for granted. Displeasure and childishness brought about by gluttony, easy victories, or perceived injustice. To surrender purity and joy for short-term stability and abundance. The pillar of regret. Luxury, defensiveness, the end of a success, and the realization of personal restrictions and limits.

Ill-dignified: Indifference, closed-mindedness, and/or isolation. To care too much about your own feelings, and ignoring the needs of others. Restlessness.

Truman Capote (1924 – 1984) Gay American novelist, screenwriter, and socialite.

Even as a child in the South, Truman Capote wanted to be famous. He showed a talent for writing early in life and eschewed formal education in favor of real-life experience.

Success came easily – his short stories were picked up by magazines, and his first novel, *Other Voices, Other Rooms,* was a hit. His most famous works are *Breakfast at Tiffany's* – which was adapted for the well-known film – and *In Cold Blood*, about the murder of a small-town family, thereby creating the genre of non-fiction novel. Capote befriended the murderers and was widely criticized for exploiting a tragic situation and fabricating quotes to sensationalize the story.

In addition to being a highly talented writer Capote was a skilled self-publicist. He enjoyed being seen at the best places with the hippest people. In later life, he became addicted to alcohol and drugs, his creative output shrunk, and he became a recluse.

Truman Capote, the Four of Cups, favored the shallower pleasures of life. Easy success, extravagance and a love of luxury paved the way to seclusion, addiction, and self-destructiveness.

FOUR OF CUPS

FIVE OF CUPS

Frustration, misfortune, and sorrow. A situation in which you expect to be delighted but end up rejected and treated unkindly, most likely from friends or loved ones. Trying, and failing, to substitute tenuous footing and a shaky defense with a blind chance at pleasure. The gateway to sadness. Regret, and having your spirit crushed, but failure to see the good you still possess.

Ill-dignified: Acceptance of what you don't have, forgiveness toward trespassers, and/or being able to move on. To be able to jump back into life after a period of rest and relaxation. The need to escape your past.

Mercedes de Acosta (1883 – 1968) Lesbian American novelist, playwright, poet, and Casanova.

Mercedes de Acosta was, it would seem, a highly charismatic woman. In addition to being physically beautiful she was sophisticated, charming, and loved to live life to the fullest. Despite limited success as a writer, Mercedes managed to connect with many of the best-known women artists of her day. She is reputed to have said she could take any woman away from any man. Her list of conquests is impressive – Greta Garbo (The Hermit), Marlene Dietrich (Queen of Wands), Isadora Duncan, Alla Nazimova, and many others. She published a controversial name-dropping autobiography, *Here Lies the Heart* and lost many friends as a result. She died alone in poverty aged 75.

To some, Mercedes de Acosta is a fame-hungry, kiss-and-tell flirt with no great talent. But to many she is a lesbian who defied the conventions of her time. Refusing to be limited by sexism and homophobia, she proudly took control of her sexuality.

Frustrated and rejected by loved ones despite her best efforts, Mercedes is sadly the Five of Cups. A great lover whose spirit was crushed in her pursuit of pleasure and happiness.

FIVE OF CUPS

SIX OF CUPS

Sexual pleasure, romance, and effortlessness. A realization that one's earlier sources of happiness are indeed the best, or to return to truths and loves that you once held near. To substitute disappointment and loss with contentment and fulfillment. The bridge between honesty and innocence. Beauty without maturity, harmony without effort, and/or lust without shame.

Ill-dignified: Conceit, presumptuousness, and rudeness. To still see yourself as in your glory days, failing to realize the truths about your losses and shortcomings. Petrification.

Joey Stefano (1968 – 1994) Gay American pornographic actor known as the original 'hungry bottom' porn star.

Born Nicholas Anthony Iacona in Philadelphia, Joey Stefano started making porn aged twenty-one. He would go on to make fifty-eight porn movies during his brief career. In addition to his good looks, Joey brought sexiness and magnetism to his performances. He was one of the first 'hungry bottoms' – men with an insatiable appetite who clearly enjoy bottoming and are verbally demanding of their partners. Up to that point, porn stars were usually 'straight acting' and almost never vocally effusive. Joey became so famous that Madonna used him not only in her video for "Deeper and Deeper" but also in her infamous *Sex* book.

Joey Stefano was rumored to be the escort of several high-profile entertainment industry figures, most notably music producer David Geffen. He was also known as a heavy drug user. At just 26 years of age, Joey Stefano overdosed on a speedball in an LA hotel room. A bottom who died at the top of his game.

Proud of being a hungry bottom and finding fulfillment in sexual pleasure, Joey Stefano is the Six of Cups. His honest and innocent way with sex exemplifies lust without shame.

SIX OF CUPS

SEVEN OF CUPS

Depravity, amorality, and escapism. Potentials, promises, relationships and/or love squandered by indulging in fantasies, drugs/alcohol and self-destructive behavior. To erroneously believe you're a success in life, or to have created a warped philosophy in order to justify your own shortcomings. The wheel of illusion. Coming to the realization that your life is riddled with delusion and constant intoxication, and often teetering on the verge of madness.

Ill-dignified: Anger, vanity, and pathological lying. To be poisonous to others, psychopathic and without any guilt or empathy. Can mean violence directed at those who threaten your illusions.

William S. Burroughs (1914 – 1997) American essayist, novelist, performer, and visual artist.

William S. Burroughs was born into a prominent and wealthy family. Rejecting propriety, he dabbled in the criminal and sexual underworlds acquiring a heroin addiction that would last a lifetime. In 1950, Burroughs shot his wife in a drunken bar game in Mexico. To avoid conviction, he lied, bribed witnesses and officials and ultimately fled the country. He then spent years in Tangiers where heroin was cheap, and sex was easy.

Burroughs parlayed his life into a series of successful novels. *Junkie*, *Queer*, and *Naked Lunch* present his personal experiences sometimes through the filter of a heroin haze or 'Interzone', as he termed it. His writings often include explicit gay sex scenes. In 1974, Burroughs returned to the US and tried unsuccessfully to teach creative writing. In later years he became a counterculture figure, featured in recordings of spoken word performances.

William S Burroughs' amorality and addictions wove a delusional web. Like the Seven of Cups, his life was characterized by intoxication, deception, and madness.

SEVEN OF CUPS

EIGHT OF CUPS

To lose interest in life or in matters that once meant much to you, or to abandon materiality and success as a reaction to failure/loss in love or relationships. Always complaining, wanting what you don't and cannot have, and to become unpleasant to be around as a result. To move from deviance and illusion into stoicism and indolence. Finding yourself too scared to feel, too angry at others you hold responsible for your emotional state, and being in denial about your own choices which led you to that state.

Ill-dignified: To be utterly without roots, wandering aimlessly without beliefs, home and/or love. Missing out on life, hoarding, and/or fearing intimacy. No spirit left.

Djuna Barnes (1892 – 1982) Lesbian American writer, illustrator, and journalist.

Djuna Barnes started writing as a journalist and illustrator in New York in 1912. Her highly personal accounts of subjects and her willingness to put herself in danger (she allowed herself to be force-fed for an article on the technique being used on hunger-striking suffragettes) brought huge success. During the 1920s and 30s, she based herself in Paris and her interviews and sketches of famous writers and artists strengthened her reputation. Her novels, including *Ryder* and *Nightwood*, were widely praised by critics and other writers. Her book *Ladies Almanack* is still argued about to this day - is it a celebration or biting critique of high society lesbian cliques?

In 1940 Djuna Barnes returned to live in New York's Greenwich Village. She now drank heavily and was broke. She hadn't published any journalism in years and relied on hand-outs from friends. Her alcoholism prevented her from writing, and she became a recluse – suspicious and argumentative. She died alone and in poverty in a small apartment. Here, she lived out the last 42 years of her life.

Although once very successful and stable, Djuna lost interest in her career and in the world. This sense of indolence associated with the Eight of Cups brought her poverty and emotional isolation.

EIGHT OF CUPS

NINE OF CUPS

Happiness tried and tested, pleasure in the little things, and utter comfort. Having the love life or relationship you've always wanted and having the wisdom to appreciate it every day, knowing that interference (or an end) could come at any time. To come to the realization that love, health and the bonds of community are the three most important things in life. Finding joy in sex, finding joy in being carefree, finding joy in the presence of others. Not letting the pains and horrors of the world get in the way of your humanist view of it.

Ill-dignified: Smugness, vanity, gluttony and/or constant dissatisfaction with everything. To pursue the desire for sensual stimulation too far, too fast. Sex addiction.

William Haines (1900 – 1973) Gay American Hollywood movie actor and acclaimed interior designer.

William Haines was one of Hollywood's rising stars in the mid-1920s. In 1926, Haines met Jimmie Shields and they became partners. He was in the top five box office earners by 1930 after making a successful transition to sound. However, following Haines' arrest for having sex in an L.A. YMCA, he was given an ultimatum by studio head, Louis B. Mayer: choose between a 'lavender marriage' and continue his movie career or stay with Jimmie and be fired. Haines chose Jimmie and they stayed together for almost fifty years.

Billy Haines and Jimmie Shields then established an interior design and antiques business. Their clients included many of Hollywood's A-listers, including Joan Crawford and Gloria Swanson. Billy died of lung cancer at age 73. Soon after, Jimmie overdosed on pills. He simply couldn't go on without Billy.

William Haines lived a happy life. He placed his relationship above movie stardom. As the Nine of Cups, he was wise enough to choose love, health, and community.

NINE OF CUPS

TEN OF CUPS

Neutral completion, bland sympathy, over-indulgence. Deep emotional abundance, but you still feel deficient, or, you've finally found love, but at the cost of your dreams and fantasies. You now know yourself, your loved ones understand you, and the things that matter most in life to you are all in order, but with lingering dissatisfaction. This card is the element of water without any other elemental balance, as far removed as possible from the divine, void of spirit, mind or body, all-surrounding and all-saturating. This is drowning. This is giving in. This is the bloating of the heart. The Ten of Cups' final lingering attribute is satiety, for regardless of the benefits that its love and bounty yield, it all ends in less than total satisfaction, albeit with the seed of a new desire, a new Ace.

Ill-dignified: A great love, friendship or passion in life given up on, or left for dead. A strong, fast passion, burning very hot and dying out very quickly. An amazing opportunity wasted.

Thom Gunn (1929 – 2004) Gay Anglo-American poet.

Born in Britain, Thom Gunn was already an established poet when he moved to the US in 1954. Initially favoring traditional verse forms, in time he employed more free verse.

Through the 1960s and '70s, his now critically acclaimed poetry came to focus on the sex & drugs underworld of San Francisco's Haight Ashbury, where he lived for many years.

His collections include *Jack Straw's Castle*, *The Passages of Joy* and most famously, *The Man with Night Sweats*, which addresses the terror caused by AIDS. Despite his highly charged sex and drug lifestyle he stayed HIV-negative.

Gunn won many awards throughout his life including the very prestigious and lucrative McArthur and Guggenheim fellowships. Money from later fellowships was used to fund his methamphetamine habit. Thom chose to live out the end of his life the same as always – immersed in drugs and sex. His final collection, *Boss Cupid*, published in 2000, explores this experience.

Success failed to satisfy Thom Gunn and his excesses. Like the Ten of Cups, he drowned in an ocean of emotions and desire.

TEN OF CUPS

PRINCESS OF CUPS

This card's appearance in a reading calls for an intense, sensitive and demonstrative response to the situation at hand. This Princess is reminding you to trust your gut, to stay true to your ideas, thoughts and opinions no matter how unorthodox, and to remain open to all opportunities of the heart that are coming your way. Remember to be kind and gracious to those who cross your path in this regard. The last thing you should ever do is react in a coarse manner. Be sweet. Be soft. Stay true to yourself.

Ill-dignified: If surrounded by too many Wands and/or Fire-based Major Arcana, this card is warning you against severe self-abuse, self-centeredness, and/or being dangerously lavish.

Dusty Springfield (1939 – 1999) Acclaimed British lesbian pop and soul singer.

During the 1960's Dusty Springfield was the queen of blue-eyed soul. Songs like "I Only Want to Be with You", "You Don't Have to Say You Love Me," and "Son of a Preacher Man" were critical and commercial successes on both sides of the Atlantic. Her distinctive bouffant hairstyle and heavy 'panda eye' makeup made her instantly recognizable. With her soulful, breathy voice and emotional interpretations, she is considered one of the greatest female vocalists of all time.

Despite this, her career stumbled in the early 1970s. Disputes with record executives and a desire to live away from the prying eyes of the media, forever curious about her sexuality, caused her to put her career on hold in the mid-70s. Her alcoholism and drug dependency made it hard for her to restart. It was a 1987 collaboration with the Pet Shop Boys that brought Dusty back to the limelight and ensured her standing as a gay icon.

Dusty's sensitive and emotional interpretations of songs endeared her to millions. She sang about being strong in the face of heartache. Her sweet and gracious public side existed alongside an addictive, self-centered personal life, making her the perfect Princess of Cups.

PRINCESS OF CUPS

PRINCE OF CUPS

This card's appearance in a reading announces an environment of revelatory responses, emotional intelligence, strong passions, and possibly intense secrets. You will find yourself perceived as a change-maker, a congenial innovator with many wishes for a different future, or you will meet someone of younger spirit, mind or age, who is rocking the boat in this manner. Regardless, this is a time of new excitements, stimulations, and values, so enjoy the novelty of it while it lasts.

Ill-dignified: If surrounded by too many Wands and/or Fire-based Major Arcana, this card is a harbinger of snake oil and Svengalis. Beware of being easily persuaded, reckless, or blind to the immediate danger.

Joe Orton (1933 – 1967) Gay British playwright and novelist.

Born to working-class parents, Joe Orton attended the Royal Academy of Dramatic Art on scholarship, where he met Kenneth Halliwell. The two became lovers. After graduating, the couple lived together and collaborated on various unsuccessful writing projects.

Although they were imprisoned for six months for modifying library book covers with salacious images and blurbs, it was this experience in prison that helped Orton find his unique voice. By the early sixties, he was writing plays without Kenneth's collaboration.

Joe Orton's plays (notably *Loot* and *Entertaining Mr. Sloan*) were written to provoke shock and outrage in the more socially conservative theatre critics and the public. Their irreverent, dark, and farcical humor won over audiences and garnered awards. Halliwell became threatened by Orton's success and jealous of his sexual adventurousness. He murdered Joe and then killed himself in their small London apartment.

Joe Orton's spirited, playful way of holding a mirror up to the establishment's hypocrisy rocked the boat in an exciting and novel way, making him an excellent Prince of Cups.

PRINCE OF CUPS

QUEEN OF CUPS

This card's appearance in a reading indicates a time to be reflective, to stop and pay attention to your dreams, and to re-introduce imagination into your life. You find that you are increasingly sensitive, not just to your physical environment, but also to the suffering of others, or you will meet someone of older heart, mind or age who is virtuous, loyal, and whose sensitivities are exceptionally acute. Having the knowledge that you yearn for, they represent the person whom you desire to be when you mature further. This card heralds the coming of tranquility and calm, and it can also represent a period of your life during which you shut yourself off from the world.

Ill-dignified: If surrounded by too many Wands or Fire-based Major Arcana, this card is a warning against manipulation and deception by friends and lovers, and/or intense insecurity and co-dependency.

Elizabeth Bishop (1911 – 1979) Lesbian American poet who became U.S. Poet Laureate.

During her early childhood, Elizabeth's father died, and her mother was taken into psychiatric care. Raised by relatives, she was often ill and spent much of her early life feeling isolated. While travelling in South America during her adult life, she met Lota de Macedo Soares, with whom she formed an intense twelve-year relationship.

Unfortunately, this relationship became unstable towards the end. Bishop was very self contained – she rarely used details of her own life as material for her poems and spoke of her personal life only in private correspondence. Bishop's poems instead focus intensely on the minutiae of everyday experience. Although she published a relatively small body of work, she managed to win the Pulitzer Prize, and the National Book Award.

Sensitive and reflective, Elizabeth Bishop was loyal to her friends and private in her relationships. She lived the Queen of Cup's life of tranquil seclusion with occasional bouts of instability and insecurity.

QUEEN OF CUPS

KING OF CUPS

This card's appearance in a reading indicates a time to recognize the traits of compassion, tolerance, and diplomacy within yourself, and to become a friendly, enthusiastic mentor towards those around you in need of nurturing. You've been graced with qualities that many around you are missing, so it's up to you to be unselfish and to be an outgoing yet caring healer and therapist for those drawn to your energies. However, you want to be careful not to be dilettantish in your applications, as many could be depending on you to be honest and truthfully loving. So long as you don't let your sensitivities get the better of you, and you maintain your warm-heartedness, you'll find that you can learn a lot about yourself from helping those in need.

Ill-dignified: If surrounded by too many Wands or Fire-based Major arcana, this card becomes the embodiment of the Devil/idle-hands situation, and can lead to depression, drug abuse, and being exposed as someone of questionable character, or with no character at all.

Alvin Ailey (1931 – 1989) Gay American choreographer, dancer, director, and activist.

Alvin Ailey was born into the segregated southern U.S. during the Great Depression, where his experiences of racism, violence and poverty were formative. At the age of 11, and soon after moving to Los Angeles, he enrolled in the multi-racial Lester Horton Dance Company. Horton was a huge influence on Ailey, introducing him to a wide range of dance styles and allowing him to experiment and develop his own style.

Following Lester Horton's death in 1953, Ailey moved to New York City and soon established his own dance troupe, The Alvin Ailey American Dance Theatre. Success came quickly with *Revelations,* a work depicting the movement of African-Americans from slavery to freedom, incorporating traditional spirituals and blues. He always insisted the troupe be multi-racial and assigned roles on the basis of a dancer's skill only. He died of AIDS aged 58.

Taking what he learned from his early teachers, he developed his own style and became a mentor to others. As the King of Cups, he brought his gifts of compassion and caring to portray the painful legacy of racism in America and to facilitate healing.

KING OF CUPS

ACE OF SWORDS

Innovation, activity, and triumph. A cutting through of ruinous concepts and ideas, thereby creating a new clarity. To substitute decay and confusion by means of precision and authority. The crown of ideas. Consciousness-raising, invoked force, and truth.

Ill-dignified: Messiness, pandemonium, and mental affliction. To be destroyed by one's own inaction. Desire for self-punishment. Wasted intelligence.

Karl Heinrich Ulrichs (1825 – 1895) Gay German activist (creator of the earliest gay rights movement), journalist, lawyer, and writer.

Karl Heinrich Ulrichs was the first person to document and name homosexuality in a new context. In the 1860s, he published a series of essays describing same-sex attraction and love, coining the terms *Uranian* (male) and *Dionian* (female) before the word 'homosexual' was first used in 1869. He spoke out publicly for the repeal of anti-gay laws and was often arrested, albeit for his words rather than for sexual offenses.

Ulrichs' 1870 statement asserting gay rights, *Araxes: A Call to Free the Nature of the Urning from Penal Law*, remains surprisingly relevant over 150 years later. Spurned in his time, Ulrichs is today honored with street names, festivals and annual awards. He is sometimes considered the first modern gay man in history.

While in much of the world today we have mostly moved beyond the call for recognition and tolerance, the modern queer sensibility originates with the ideas of Karl Heinrich Ulrichs. He is the Ace of Swords, cutting through old certainties and seeding new ideas. He raised the world's consciousness by being the first to clearly articulate the new truth.

ACE OF SWORDS

TWO OF SWORDS

Objectivity, compromises, and the need for keen perception. A stalemate that is kept until enough thought and care have been put into a decision. To substitute ambiguity and dependency with peace of mind and equilibrium. The seed of reflection.

Ill-dignified: A state of mind characterized by difficult choices, concessions, and a search for truth. A balancing act between your own beliefs and those of others and/or the establishment. Indecision, bewilderment, near-sightedness.

Roberta Cowell (1918 – 2011) British trans woman racing driver and fighter pilot.

Roberta Cowell's early life was filled with macho adventure. An RAF pilot shot down during WWII, Cowell was held as a prisoner of war in Germany. After the war, she became a competitive race car driver. However, a combination of depression resulting from gender discord and PTSD made life very unhappy, and by 1952, Roberta began her transition. She came to realize that her unconscious mind was predominantly female. She took action and underwent Britain's first successful gender reassignment surgery.

In 1954, her story was published in a UK magazine, and for a time, she was a press sensation. Cowell continued to race cars and fly planes. In 1957, she won the Shelsley Walsh Speed Hill Climb, one of the oldest racing titles in the world and eventually clocked over 1600 flying hours. She was in her 90s when she died.

A process of reflection produced a keener and more objective self-image for Roberta Cowell. As the Two of Swords, her difficult choices broke an identity stalemate and brought her a sense of personal equilibrium.

TWO OF SWORDS

THREE OF SWORDS

Deception, restriction, and secrecy. A dark episode of mental anguish brought about by either a rejection by others, obstacles to self-expression, or a grievous personal loss. To lose an uneasy peace due to dangerous conflicts and extreme doubts. The house of depression and chaos. To go through a gauntlet of pain in order to find relief, or perhaps, to find a perverse delight in what shouldn't be considered pleasure.

Ill-dignified: Optimism, forgiveness and finding joy where you never have before. To let go of pain and melancholy and accept who/where you are. A reconciliation with one who has done you a terrible wrong.

Stephen Donaldson (1946 – 1996) American bisexual LGBT rights and prison reform activist.

Stephen Donaldson was a lifelong agitator who seemed to spend most of his time in conflict with authorities of one sort or another. It's not surprising then that he became known as Donny the Punk. Beginning at Columbia University, Donaldson founded a gay rights group, the Student Homophile League, that drew opposition from both College authorities *and* the Mattachine Society, founded by Harry Hay (The Hierophant). He felt ostracized by the gay liberation movement because of his bisexuality. Later, he was discharged from the Navy for sexual misconduct.

Arrested following a series of 'pray-ins' at the White House opposing the Vietnam war, Donaldson refused bail and was jailed. Here he was orally and anally raped by a group of prisoners with the collusion of the prison guards. Despite a history of depression, panic attacks and attempted suicide, Donny the Punk led a prison reform movement and raised awareness about prison rape.

Rejected by others and driven into dark periods of mental anguish, Stephen Donaldson is the Three of Swords. Moving through depression, pain, and chaos, he ultimately found liberation.

THREE OF SWORDS

FOUR OF SWORDS

Recovery, a resulting new dogma, and/or a change for the better. A quiet respite, or a truce with enemies, following much sorrow, chaos and possible sickness. To substitute disobedience and anxiety with succor and contemplation. The pillar of peace. Convention, conciliation, and the establishment of a new intellectual authority.

Ill-dignified: Exhaustion, evasion and/or frustration from a lack of improvement. To have your mind utterly out of step with your body, often due to indolence. The avoidance of what needs to be done.

Richard Isay (1934 – 2012) Gay American activist, author, psychiatrist, and psychoanalyst.

Richard Isay was both a practitioner and a teacher of psychiatry and psychoanalysis. Highly successful in these fields, he was an active and openly gay member of the *American Psychiatric Association* and the *American Psychoanalytic Association*; early on in his activism work he sometimes addressed professional conferences wearing a facemask. His book *Being Homosexual: Gay Men and Their Development,* presented the first non-pathological explanation of the development of homosexuality. Up to that time homosexuality had been thought of as a mental illness that could be treated and cured. He argued that homosexuality is a normal variant of sexual identity, and that psychoanalysts should stop trying to change the sexual orientation of their patients. He considered such practice injurious and argued that homosexuality is an inborn identity. As a result of Richard Isay's work, the psychiatric profession removed homosexuality from its list of mental illnesses.

Isay was also an early champion of gay marriage and a firm believer in queer peoples' need for romantic love. He led the psychiatric world to eventually embrace same-sex marriage.

Richard Isay is the Four of Swords who challenged the old dogma of illness and anxiety, replacing it with a new intellectual authority emphasizing health, calm and diversity.

FOUR OF SWORDS

FIVE OF SWORDS

Meanness, failure, and humiliation. A dangerous battle in which you could suffer a grave defeat at the hands of those out to disrupt and destroy. To substitute a respite and comfort with a chance to assist friends, and failing. The gateway to slander. The severance of bonds, the weakness that comes from being alone, and/or the grieving that comes with it.

Ill-dignified: Resentment over past events, and the lingering pain of a wound, accompanied by a strong desire to put it behind you. To be followed by a conflict or contentious person despite your attempts to flee. The need to ignore others.

Roger Casement (1864 – 1916) Gay Anglo-Irish diplomat, humanitarian, poet and revolutionary.

As a diplomat stationed in the Belgian Congo, Roger Casement exposed the extreme brutality, racism and imperialist excesses used in harvesting rubber. He was knighted by the British government following his report on the situation. He subsequently detailed severe abuses against the Putumayo people in the Peruvian Amazon. Casement became an international ambassador for human rights. However, when he turned his attention to British imperialism in his native Ireland, the ruling establishment quickly turned against him.

Captured by the British following a failed attempt to import German guns for use in the 1916 Easter Uprising, Casement was tried for treason. Given his status and reputation most expected he would be imprisoned rather than executed. However, the authorities leaked excerpts from his personal diaries describing his sexual activities with men, causing public opinion to turn against him. He was executed by hanging.

Public humiliation undermined Roger Casement's heroic activism. As the Five of Swords, he was defeated by slander and malice.

FIVE OF SWORDS

SIX OF SWORDS

Neutrality, achieving goals by use of the intellect, and/or relief from professional pressures. A rough, perhaps painful transition, from sorrowful times into peaceful ones, and/or from a set of narrow beliefs into a system of more objective knowing. To substitute depression and grief with analytical thinking and balance. The bridge between science and clarity. Shamelessly admitting previous errors, moving forward with new works and labors, and/or seeing oneself as a part of humanity.

Ill-dignified: Selfishness, pride and stubbornness. To assume that your shortcomings are the same as everyone else's. Always making excuses.

Alfred Kinsey (1894 – 1956) Bisexual American sexologist and founder of the Institute for Sex Research, now known as the Kinsey Institute.

Dr. Alfred Kinsey was a pioneer in the study of human sexuality. In *Sexual Behavior in the Human Male,* he introduces the 6-point Kinsey scale of sexual orientation – 0 denoting exclusively hetero, 6 denoting exclusively homo. In *Sexual Behavior and the Human Female,* he debunked the old notion that women are less sexual. This early work opened the way for a serious, objective approach to the study of sex. The Kinsey reports were read by millions of people and reshaped how we understand sexuality.

Kinsey himself was bisexual and promoted a sex-positive attitude among his colleagues and subjects. He became a public face of the sexual revolution of the 1950s and '60s, and his ideas entered popular culture. However, some of the practices used in preparing his research proved controversial - having sex with his assistants, filming subjects during sex in his home, and fudging source data.

For millions of people Alfred Kinsey's work changed their life. By moving from depression and grief to science and clarity, Kinsey is the Six of Swords, showing us that we all exist within the spectra of human sexuality.

SIX OF SWORDS

Uselessness, instability, and fascination with artifice. Deciding to give up a long-standing belief or way of thinking for ignoble reasons: a lazy lack of energy, a desire to appease or to pursue a pipe dream. To be given a situation/opportunity to mature, but to treat it suspiciously, and likely respond with deception and cynicism. The wheel of futility. Coming to the realization that you can get away with everything in life, avoid everything in life, and somehow create sympathy from others by means of your warped charisma.

Ill-dignified: Having little success from much mental effort. Surrendering to fate and realizing the need to break from old habits before it's too late. Giving up on life.

Arthur Rimbaud (1854 – 1891) Gay French poet, explorer and libertine, whose work is considered a forerunner to modernism, surrealism, and symbolism.

Arthur Rimbaud's talent for living and for art blossomed early. At sixteen years old he chose to dedicate his life to the "derangement of the senses" – to cultivate a true poetic vision. He started drinking, stealing, and became a vagrant, believing that these experiences would sharpen his artistic sensibility. Rimbaud soon produced ingenious works, including *A Season in Hell* and *Illuminations*. His poetry influenced many and is a precursor to surrealism.

At seventeen years of age Rimbaud moved to Paris and began a tempestuous affair with the married poet Paul Verlaine. Both writers abandoned their responsibilities and binged on absinthe and drugs. At one point Verlaine shot Rimbaud in a drunken rage. They eventually split up and Rimbaud joined the Dutch colonial army to further his search for experience. After travels in Indonesia, where he deserted and fled into the jungle, he ended up in Yemen and Ethiopia as a coffee trader in Harar, and a gun runner for Menelik II. In his late thirties Arthur Rimbaud died of bone cancer.

Rimbaud's search for a primitive pipe dream caused him to neglect his civilized talent. His futile pursuit of an idealized poetic life typifies the Seven of Swords.

SEVEN OF SWORDS

Remoteness, imprisonment, and/or blindly following a law, rule or way of thinking. Doing the supposed right thing in life when it's actually running contrary to the expression of your authentic self or staying indecisive and unsure for so long that you no longer know what's true anymore. To move from deception and futility into isolation and restriction. Finding oneself in a position to make a big difference to a cause through self-sacrifice but deciding not to because of fear or inhibitions. The need to take a leap of faith.

Ill-dignified: A time for self-acceptance, contemplation, and personal accountability. Coming clean about the past. Seeing things in a new, and better light.

Rock Hudson (1925 – 1985) Gay American film actor and one of the biggest movie stars of the Golden Age of Hollywood.

In the 1950s, Rock Hudson was box office gold. He was nominated for the Best Actor Academy Award for his role in *Giant* (1956), and the following year was named the U.S.'s favorite male movie star. He made nine films with legendary filmmaker Douglas Sirk. In the 1960s, he starred in a series of extremely popular romantic comedies, three of which co-starred Doris Day. In the 1970s, Hudson's flagging movie career was bolstered by the success of the TV show *McMillan & Wife*.

Like other gay celebrities at the time, Rock Hudson carefully hid his sexuality from his fans. Widely known in Hollywood circles as a gay man, he concealed the fact from the press and the public. However, when Hudson started showing the debilitating signs of AIDS it became harder to deny the truth. Initially claiming he had liver cancer, he finally admitted that he was suffering from the disease but said he became infected from a blood transfusion.

Rock Hudson's deception led to isolation and pain. The Eight of Swords is like a self-created prison. In the end, Rock Hudson couldn't free himself from his own fears.

EIGHT OF SWORDS

NINE OF SWORDS

Cruelty, oppression, and mental anguish. Having suffered malice at the hands of others, you have no choice but to give in to the hopelessness of the situation you find yourself in. With despair, dark cynicism and/or shame upon you, you must come to the realization of accepting the death of what you had, or else it'll get the best of you and make you a monster, a sociopath, a fanatic. You're either the victim of a spiteful, sadistic inquisitor, or you yourself are one. This is a card for blind revenge, for the deepest depressions, for nightmarish anxieties, and for using your brilliance in order to devise the most wicked of plans.

Ill-dignified: Submission, conformity, endurance. Using practicality, stoicism and responsibility to chase away the demons, the concerns, and the scares. Being too grounded to be hurt.

Andy Milligan (1929 – 1991) Gay American cult filmmaker, screenwriter and playwright.

Andy Milligan started his career as part of the Caffe Cino off-Broadway experimental theater. He started making movies in the early 1960s. The films, typically shot with a handheld 16mm camera, were morality tales, very often with horror or macabre settings. While some film critics class him as one of the worst directors ever, he has acquired a cult status. Some of his films have been lost, but many, including *Vapors*, *The Ghastly Ones*, *Seeds of Sin* and *Fleshpot on 42nd Street*, survive as outstanding examples of early queer cinema.

Milligan survived an extremely abusive childhood and youth. His mother was emotionally unstable as well as physically, mentally, and likely sexually, abusive. Milligan himself was often cruel and abusive to the people he worked with – sometimes provoking fights with financiers or humiliating actors on set. He was also a sadist sexually – some of his partners later described him as the cruelest person they had ever met. He died in abject poverty of AIDS in 1991 and is buried in an unmarked grave.

Andy Milligan, the Nine of Swords, couldn't escape the abject abuse and cruelty of his childhood. He became a horrible monster who made monstrous horror movies.

NINE OF SWORDS

TEN OF SWORDS

Death, ruin, and utter failure. Harmful events and circumstances far beyond your control, a betrayal and/or a mental crisis, a total breakdown from which there is only negativity and disruption. The loss of touch with reality, violence when backed into a corner, and/or the stinging to death of oneself. This card is the element of Air without any other elemental balance, as far removed as possible from the divine, void of heart, soul or body, all-persecuting and all-destroying. The Ten of Swords ends in annihilation, the end of delusions, and all the pain that comes with it. This is collapsing. This is silence. This is death. Yet, out of this arises a new concept, a new idea. A new Ace of Swords will take root.

Ill-dignified: The realization of total defeat with the horror and pain of it made tangible. A long healing and regenerative process. Knowing and accepting that the only way is up.

Aileen Wuornos (1956 – 2002) American serial killer.

Aileen Wuornos came from an extremely dysfunctional home environment. Her father was schizophrenic and convicted of child sexual abuse. Her mother abandoned her children. Wuornos was also beaten and sexually abused by her grandfather. Kicked out of home at 15, she gave birth to a son who was surrendered for adoption. Aileen became a prostitute to support herself. She settled in Florida, where she was continually in trouble with the law for drunk driving, assault, disturbing the peace, car theft, bank robbery and resisting arrest.

She met and moved in with Tyra Moore in 1987. Between 1989 and 1990, Aileen Wournos murdered seven men. She claimed self-defense as they had tried to rape her. She was soon apprehended, and police convinced Tyra to elicit a confession from Aileen in exchange for immunity from prosecution. After ten years on death row Wournos was executed by the state of Florida.

Aileen Wournos suffered extreme damage at the hands of others. Like the Ten of Swords, her life was characterized by disruption, negativity, and ruin, ending in her own annihilation.

TEN OF SWORDS

PRINCESS OF SWORDS

This card's appearance in a reading means that now is the time when your ideas and mental acuity are supreme. You're currently in a state when your skills of logic and no-nonsense wisdom are at their most decisive and aggressive pitch. Do not second-guess yourself now, as you're in complete control. Although your ideas may seem wild and caustic to some, they cut to the heart of the matter like no one else's.

Ill-dignified: If surrounded by too many Discs and/or Earth-based Major Arcana, this card heralds plans falling apart, ambitions thwarted, and the inability to clearly express your ideas. At worst, it's a fateful reminder that you'll never make your dreams manifest.

Valerie Solanas (1936 – 1988) Lesbian American radical feminist – the woman who shot Andy Warhol.

As a teenager, Valerie Solanas ran away from an unstable and abusive family home in New Jersey. Despite these early disadvantages she graduated from the University of Maryland and studied at Berkeley, where she wrote the *SCUM Manifesto*, her best-known work. SCUM, an acronym for *Society for Cutting Up Men*, was a call to radical action, including the overthrow of the government, the abolition of money and the elimination of the male sex.

Returning to New York, Valerie passed her play *Up Your Ass* to Andy Warhol (King of Coins), asking him to produce it. Although Warhol misplaced this only copy, Solanas quickly accused Warhol of being part of the system of oppression and of stealing her work. In a fit of paranoia, she shot and seriously injured Warhol. She served two years in a psychiatric institution for the shooting.

To some, Valerie Solanas is a feminist heroine engaged in radical thought and direct action, while others focus on her mental illness. Either way, she is the Princess of Swords – her insight and wisdom were translated decisively and aggressively even if these events resulted in a thwarting of her ambitions. Failing to express her ideas sufficiently well with words, she resorted to a calamitous course, which was her undoing.

PRINCESS OF SWORDS

PRINCE OF SWORDS

This card's appearance in a reading heralds a time when impetuousness, articulation, and forward-thinking assist you in taking a stand on your ideas and decisions. You may also soon encounter an intellectual situation in which a clever mind and domineering actions will result in a great boon, or you will meet someone of younger spirit, mind or age who is incredibly confident, casually eccentric, and brave, who will inspire you to believe that what you suspect to be true is in fact, true. Now is the time to ride into the debate-battle in the way you've always dreamed, as your words are as sharp as they've ever been.

Ill-dignified: If surrounded by too many Discs and/or Earth-based Major Arcana, this card is a warning against knee-jerk impulsivity and fanaticism, or a risk of coming across as intellectually erratic and/or a devil's advocate.

Pier Paolo Pasolini (1922 – 1975) Gay Italian filmmaker, writer and intellectual famous for his highly controversial movies.

Born in the traditionally leftist city of Bologna, Pasolini was a sometime member of the Communist Party but was also highly critical of its policies. The party welcomed the high-profile intellectual but disliked his open homosexuality. Highly regarded as a poet he started making movies in 1961 with *Accattone*, an unromantic but sympathetic look at Rome's petty criminal class. His greatest works, including *The Gospel According to Matthew* and *Salo, or the 120 Days of Sodom,* are among the most controversial films ever made.

Pasolini never held back in articulating his criticisms of bourgeois institutions nor of the power of the Catholic Church and the post-war consumerism destroying traditional Italian society. He was murdered in 1975 by a seventeen-year-old prostitute. His murder is commonly believed to have been a mafia-style execution ordered by anti-communists.

Intellectually fearless, Pasolini exemplifies the Prince of Swords with his clear and articulate challenge to established beliefs and behaviors. His youthful transgression of established mores is both exciting and unsettling.

PRINCE OF SWORDS

QUEEN OF SWORDS

This card's appearance in a reading announces a time to be poised, self-assured, and observational – also rational and full of tact. You will realize that you need to be a person of seemingly extreme individualisms and radical new ideas in order to achieve your ends, or you will meet someone of older heart, mind or age who is righteous, free-thinking, and highly intellectual. They know the answers you seek and can help you accomplish your goals without much trouble, as long as you follow them to the letter. Nevertheless, this card heralds confidence, grace and emotional control. You recognize your ideas as being the best ideas for the matter at hand.

Ill-dignified: If surrounded by too many Discs or Earth-based Major Arcana, this card is a warning against aloofness, isolation, and/or unreliability of speech.

Audre Lorde (1934 – 1992) Lesbian American writer, radical feminist, and activist.

Born into a family of Caribbean immigrants, Audre became estranged from them after high school. Her early poetry reflects her interest in the peace movement, the civil rights movement, and the feminist movement. Later, she explored her multiple identities or affinities – black, woman, lesbian – refusing to be boxed into any single one. She demanded to be acknowledged in terms of all these intersecting identities. She angered many white feminists by pointing out the racism inherent in its normative view.

Rather than define women simply in opposition to men, Audre insisted that differences between women be given focus. Lorde challenged the traditionally middle-class, white feminist movement with new perspectives on race and sexuality.

Audre Lorde is the Queen of Swords because she articulated her individual truth with confidence, grace, and emotional control – always recognizing the power of her ideas. She died following a prolonged battle with cancer, taking the name Gamba Adisa or Warrior: She Who Makes Her Meaning Known.

QUEEN OF SWORDS

KING OF SWORDS

This card's appearance in a reading indicates a time to recognize the traits of a certain cleverness and keen, scholastic adroitness within yourself and to be an advocate for your innovative ideas for which you are now very certain. Your way of thinking is theoretical, conceptual if you will, but it is the result of years of self-analysis and discipline. This is a time to stand your well-deserved ground, to wield the sword of your strong, new insights, and to slay the hindering old ways of thinking. This is not a time to reflect, but to know that your intellectual power is at its strongest and most insightful, and your just criticisms of others at their sharpest.

Ill-dignified: If surrounded by too many Discs or Earth-based Major Arcana, this card is a warning against deceiving others, tyranny over your loved ones, and/or excessive, unwarranted judgments.

Robert Duncan (1919 – 1988) Gay American poet and public figure, one of the earliest writers to come out publicly in the U.S.

Robert Duncan was adopted and raised by a devout Theosophist couple in 1920 who selected him on the basis of his astrological birth chart. He grew up with a strong sense of an esoterically defined destiny. Active in the pre-Stonewall gay rights movement, he wrote and signed the influential 1944 essay *The Homosexual in Society,* comparing the gay rights struggle with those of African Americans and Jews. Such a public declaration was almost unheard of at the time.

Basing himself in San Francisco, Duncan became a central figure in the city's fertile literary scene. His highly creative poetry often draws upon Western esoteric symbols and structures to express universal mythopoetic themes. He is cited as an inspiration by many who followed and is sometimes referred to as a poet's poet; however Duncan's work has often been criticized for being too intellectual and lacking feeling. He died in 1988, leaving behind Jess Collins, his lover of 37 years, who was also an accomplished artist in his own right.

Duncan's intellectual brilliance and personal leadership make him an ideal King of Swords. His insight, understanding and highly developed sense of Self meant he asserted himself in the world with few doubts.

KING OF SWORDS

ACE OF COINS

Recognition, prosperity, and luck. The discovery of a singular new wealth atop a mountain of previous treasures. To substitute corruption and exploitation with courage and a fresh start. The crown of labor. New opportunities, new shapes, new forms, new paradigms.

Ill-dignified: Missing your chance, bad planning, and lacking foresight. To not get out of the way of obvious destruction. Manipulation of results.

Magnus Hirschfeld (1868 – 1935) Gay Jewish-German physician and sexologist.

Magnus Hirschfeld devoted his life to understanding gay sexuality. He gathered a vast archive and extensive research library within his *Institute for Sexual Research,* which opened in 1919. The Institute also housed medical and educational services, was a base for advocacy work internationally, and provided refuge to many artists, intellectuals and politicians. So respected was the Institute and Hirschfeld that he became known as the 'Einstein of Sex'.

In 1933 the Nazi party assumed power in Germany, and almost immediately, the Institute, along with its archive and library, was destroyed. Hirschfeld's life work went up in flames. He himself was out of the country and set up home as an exile in Paris where he died soon after on his sixty-seventh birthday in 1935.

Hirschfeld assembled a new and unique treasure trove of information on human sexuality. A true Ace of Coins, he labored to mine this wealth of information, and in so doing, created a paradigm shift in society's perception of sexuality. Yet he nearly failed to get out of the way of its (and potentially, his own) destruction at the hands of the Nazis.

ACE OF COINS

Vacillation and adaptability. A predictable alteration between extremes, opposites, or differing elements, kept balanced by effort and work. To substitute making-do and thoughtlessness with integration and candidness. The seed of change. The ebb and flow of physical and material factors in one's life, including changes to your body, job, home, travel and marital status.

Ill-dignified: Abandonment, over-commitment, and ineptitude. To be in a panic over finances, home life, and status. An unending state of anxiety.

Alan L. Hart (1890–1962) American trans man novelist, physician, and radiologist.

Early in life Alan Hart identified strongly as male. Although biologically female, he preferred boy's clothes and traditional male activities. When he reached adulthood, Alan underwent sex change surgery - one of the earliest in the U.S. Hart legally changed his name, married his wife Inez, and set up a medical practice in Oregon. Unfortunately, he was outed on several occasions and forced to move to new cities. This led to problems in his relationship and led to an eventual divorce.

Soon after the divorce Hart found stable employment as a medical researcher treating tuberculosis, and a new, loving wife. He was a pioneer in the use of the x-ray in the early detection of disease. Hart also had a successful career as a writer, publishing four novels. In *The Undaunted,* the lead character is a gay radiologist who experiences discrimination at work and was hassled as he was forced to move from place to place.

The Two of Coins is a card of differing elements kept in balance by our hard work. Alan L. Hart managed a successful home life and a high-profile job along with a creative side. All this in the face of great prejudice and discrimination

TWO OF COINS

THREE OF COINS

Firm foundations, diligence, and hard work. Teamwork and the perfection of abilities leading to a successful manifestation of an idea. To substitute disorganization and an unwillingness to change with constructive action and successful collaboration. The house of initiation and solidity. Financial growth, personal growth, and/or the growth of a community due to cooperation and focus on a particular subject or skill.

Ill-dignified: Greed, narrow-mindedness, and banality. To fervently seek blood from a stone with a total absence of understanding. An utter lack of teamwork likely due to discord over finances.

Tom Waddell (1937 – 1987) and the Gay Games Gay American decathlete and physician who founded the Gay Games.

Tom Waddell was an athlete, a physician, and a humanitarian. He attended college on a sports scholarship and went on to graduate in medicine. With a strong sense of social justice, he attended the civil rights demonstrations in Selma, Alabama. Drafted in 1966, he expressed conscientious objections to the Vietnam War and was instead assigned to train for the 1968 Mexico Olympic Games. He participated in the games, but a 1972 knee injury ended his sports career.

Waddell created the first Gay Games, held in San Francisco in 1982. The US Olympic Committee objected to the original name, the Gay Olympics, and sued Waddell. With a strong emphasis on sportsmanship, personal achievement, and inclusiveness the games were and continue to be a huge success. Gay Games XI, held in 2023, was co-hosted by Hong Kong and Guadalajara. Gay Games XII will take place in Valencia, Spain in 2026.

With success built on teamwork and organization, Tom Waddell and the Gay Games are the Three of Coins. Their focus and skill have added great value to the global LGBT community.

THREE OF COINS

FOUR OF COINS

Earthly dominance, adherence to laws, and material influence. An astonishing amount of hard work, perhaps done by others, and for which the credit is erroneous. To substitute selfishness and strife with tradition and security. The pillar of power. Materialism, conservatism, and the need to possess and control one's environment.

Ill-dignified: Narrow-mindedness, suspicion and/or looking to others for a sense of aesthetics. To become a shut-in and obsessed with self-protection at all costs. The overuse of every resource available.

Malcolm Forbes (1919 – 1990) American entrepreneur, politician, and heir to the Forbes business fortune.

Malcolm Forbes inherited full control of *Forbes* magazine in 1964 following a brief dalliance with politics. Under his leadership the business diversified and grew significantly. He had sharp business instincts. Forbes was a strong advocate for capitalism and free markets. He also enjoyed the fruits of his labor, living a very lavish lifestyle. He collected yachts, artworks, houses, artifacts, motorcycles, and hot air balloons, among other expensive status symbols. Forbes was famous for his opulent birthday parties, which cost millions, and included many rich and powerful names on the invite list.

Following his death, Malcolm Forbes was outed. The world learned that he had led a closeted double life. This most public of men had kept his homosexuality hidden from public view.

As the Four of Coins, Malcolm Forbes commanded material, political and social power. His business acumen resulted in great authority and a deeply conservative outlook. Ultimately his narrow-mindedness and his wealth became barriers to living an open, authentic life.

FOUR OF COINS

FIVE OF COINS

Physical injury, bad investment, and financial anxiety. A disturbing situation in which you experience inaction as the result of a sudden loss of property, money, security and/or work. To substitute control and stability for a chance at more success but end up with even less than before. The gateway to poverty. Losing faith in oneself and the system, a loss of resources and/or an impending sense of isolation.

Ill-dignified: Labor moving full steam ahead, and the cultivation around a solid foundation – be it building or idea. To apply your intellect to disturbances and make them work for you. The need to devise new models.

Anthony Blunt (1907 – 1983) Gay British art historian and notorious Soviet spy.

Anthony Blunt, a distant cousin of Elizabeth Bowes-Lyon, Queen Elizabeth's mother, was recruited as a Soviet spy while studying at Cambridge University. During WWII, he was subsequently hired into British intelligence agency MI5 and became a double agent. Towards the end of the war, he was sent to Berlin to secretly destroy embarrassing letters written by the Duke of Windsor to Adolf Hitler; for this, he was knighted. Blunt was a leading scholar and art historian, publishing several books. He was also the keeper of Queen Elizabeth's personal art collection.

Blunt later came under suspicion, and in 1964 he confessed all and was promised anonymity and immunity from prosecution. For many years he continued to be part of the British Establishment. However, following her election in 1979, Prime Minister Margaret Thatcher exposed Blunt's espionage activities. He was stripped of his knighthood and publicly disgraced.

Anthony Blunt experienced a sudden loss of status and power. The Five of Coins is a card of poverty. Blunt lost everything he valued – including faith in the system.

FIVE OF COINS

SIX OF COINS

Philanthropy, gratification and benevolent influence. A situation in which one with more power, wealth and success bestows a small part of his or her fortune onto another in need of help. To substitute worry and inaction with assurance and vigilance. The bridge between hope and reward. Profits, improvements and/or the eventualities of good karma.

Ill-dignified: Cupidity, jealousy, and lies. To find oneself in serious debt and lacking a plan to pay it back. Material self-destruction.

Winnaretta Singer (1865 – 1943) Lesbian heiress to the Singer fortune, patron of the arts, and promoter of public health and social housing projects.

American-born heiress of the Singer sewing machine fortune, Winnaretta lived most of her life in Paris. She became Princesse de Polignac through her 'lavender marriage' to gay composer Edmond de Polignac. They were both music lovers and it seems they loved and respected each other very much within their marriage of convenience. Winnaretta was openly, blatantly lesbian (a rarity in the late nineteenth century) and never tried to hide her many affairs with women. Her sexuality was never a problem – for her, at least.

Winnaretta Singer-Polignac was a renowned philanthropist. She used her money to sponsor the arts, especially music. Among her beneficiaries are Kurt Weill, Erik Satie, and Igor Stravinsky. She also donated funds for public housing projects, a workers' hospital, and a nursing school. Even today, the Singer-Polignac Foundation supports projects in science, literature, the arts, and culture – primarily in France.

Using her great wealth to help others less fortunate than herself, Winnaretta Singer is the Six of Coins. Her support for the poor, and for struggling artists, rewarded their efforts and sustained their hopes.

SIX OF COINS

143

SEVEN OF COINS

Loss, promises unfulfilled, and blighted environments. Having one's hard work and brilliant planning spoiled by carelessness, idleness and/or abandonment. To dream big, develop successfully, and invest heavily, but to have the product or result be of benefit to everyone else but you. The wheel of failure. Coming to the realization that what was sowed without much planning, and involving too much risk, is doomed to reap nothing of real worth.

Ill-dignified: To do honorable work for the sake of the work itself, or for the sake of the goodness you know will come from it. A long-term plan paying off in spades. Much delay, but worth it in the long run.

Lili Elbe (1882 – 1931) Danish trans woman, painter, model and one of the earliest recipients of gender-affirming surgery.

Before transitioning, Einar Mogens Wegener was a successful painter in Denmark. He married fellow artist Gerda Gottlieb, who in the 1920s, produced many paintings of young women, often with Einar/Lili as the model. Indeed, Lili would often pass as Einar's sister. The paintings caused a sensation throughout Denmark as no one could fathom that the model was indeed Gottlieb's husband, Einar. Gottlieb later gave up painting Lili, believing it to be part of Einar's new identity, and not something to be exploited.

In 1930, Lili went to Germany to undergo sex reassignment surgery. Procedures were highly experimental, unproven, and extremely risky. Lili's case had such a high profile at the time that the Danish courts allowed an annulment of her marriage to Gottlieb. Lili also managed to change her name and registered gender. However, her fifth operation in less than two years, an attempt to transplant a uterus, failed horribly. Tragically, at almost 50 years of age, Lili died from organ rejection.

Lili dreamed of being a fully functioning biological female and risked everything for that dream. With the Seven of Coins, plans for material or physical success can meet with failure.

SEVEN OF COINS

EIGHT OF COINS

Common sense, practical use of resources, and the patience to reap at the most beneficial times. Applying wisdom towards issues regarding business, materiality, and the body, and calculating the best possible outcome without losing any creativity in the process. To move from failure and sloth into prudence and vigor. Finding that the interests/anxieties of the common people, or those that are subject to you (employees, friends who hold you in esteem), are what you should be most concerned about in your life.

Ill-dignified: Taking advantage of those in a weaker position of power. Cunningly using your skills for self-promotion and advantage. Working your fingers to the bone with nothing to show for it.

John Maynard Keynes (1883 –1946) Gay British economist and philosopher.

J.M. Keynes was one of the most highly regarded economists of the twentieth century – and thus far in the twenty-first. He promoted the idea that governments should spend money to stimulate demand for goods and services during economic downturns, thereby creating employment and prosperity. This interventionist strategy has been used many times, and as recently as 2008, following the international banking crisis, Keynes' ideas moved to the fore.

Keynes was also a member of London's Bloomsbury Group of writers and aesthetes. He believed the acquisition of money for itself to be pathological – rather, it should be used in the pursuit of pleasure. He was a strong supporter of the arts. Keynes was open about his sexuality and kept diaries of his many sexual adventures. Critics of his economic theories used his sexuality to discredit him, claiming that he had no interest in the longer-term consequences of his theories because he was childless.

Confident, successful, and virtuous, Keynes, the Eight of Coins, truly understood the nature of money and spent his wealth on arts and leisure.

EIGHT OF COINS

NINE OF COINS

Confidence, self-sufficiency, and comfort. Having achieved material success either through careful considerations, investments, being a virtuous person, and/or good luck, it is now time to create a more relaxing life. Troubles of the recent past are nearly over, so you should come to the realization that spending your winnings, enjoying leisure time, and appreciating the physical world in all its glory is the best of all possible things right now. Good management, grace and honor are to be practiced so as to not lose your bearings and/or recent gains. Don't let gains come to define you, and don't accept the increases if they entail too many decreases in other areas of life, namely love and spirituality.

Ill-dignified: Avarice, theft, duplicity. Hindrances to financial gain, or over-investment to the point of crippling the rest of your life. King Midas – all you touch turns to gold, until that's all you're left with.

Vita Sackville-West (1892 – 1962) Bisexual British aristocrat, writer and gardener who defied convention to live life on her own terms.

The daughter of a richly titled English family, Vita was provided with the best life had to offer. She married a British diplomat and travelled widely. She used her time to write prolifically (poetry, novels, and biographies) and with some critical acclaim. *The Edwardians* and *All Passion Spent* are her two works most read today. She also devoted herself to landscaping the gardens at Sissinghurst, her grand Tudor estate, now open to the public.

Although married with children, Vita had many lesbian lovers throughout her life, most notably Virginia Woolf (The Priestess). Vita and Virginia's affair was brief, but they continued to exchange love letters for many years after. Woolf's novel *Orlando* is clearly, directly inspired by Sackville-West.

Vita's appetite for life and willingness to reshape her social and physical environment make her the Nine of Coins. According to her son, Nigel Nicolson, "She fought for the right to love, men and women, rejecting the conventions that marriage demands exclusive love..."

NINE OF COINS

TEN OF COINS

Corrupt perfection, inertness, and pointless treasure. Material wealth you once only dreamed of, but feeling trapped by it, defined by it, and incapable of being seen or defined beyond it. You have prosperity, affluence, and great wisdom, but you failed to fill and complete the other parts of your soul. This card is the element of Earth without any other elemental balance, completely removed from heart, soul or mind, all-encumbered and all-corpulent. The Ten of Coins is the heaviest weight tied to the soul, keeping it utterly earthbound. This is apathy. This is indifference. This is godlessness. But, if you can let go of it all you can lightly float back up to Paradise – a new Ace of Coins sprouting from a garden's dirt, wiser for new opportunities.

Ill-dignified: Mental dullness, and loss of memory. The state of being so incapable of a decision that it affects your physical movement. Rot.

Liberace (1919 – 1987) Gay American pianist, actor, singer and extravagant entertainer known as Mr. Showmanship.

The child of working-class immigrants, Wladziu Valentino Liberace started playing piano as a child and showed great flair. At the pinnacle of his career, Liberace was the highest-paid entertainer in the world. He developed a popular style of playing classical pieces and charmed audiences with his schmaltzy persona. With his trademark candelabra, opulent furs, and gem-studded rings, he seemed classy to his millions of adoring, mostly female, fans. His seventy recordings, successful TV shows, Las Vegas residencies and many product endorsements led him very far from his humble beginnings.

Ever the showman, Liberace spent lavishly, decorating his homes with expensive antiques and outrageous features like a piano-shaped pool. He loved to display his success to the public but vociferously denied his sexuality - even suing papers if they hinted that he was gay. Politically conservative and devoutly Catholic, he died of AIDS in 1987, trying to conceal the cause of his death.

Liberace buried himself beneath a mountain of glitter and gold. Like the Ten of Coins, material excess corrupted his happiness.

TEN OF COINS

PRINCESS OF COINS

This card's appearance in a reading heralds a great opportunity for renewal, either physical or material, or it means a new beginning with your job/career, finances, or your body. If you're willing to take on the qualities of generosity, compassion and conscientiousness, these new prospects will indeed prove successful.

And take advantage of any sound offers to move to a new home, to travel or to transform your environment into what you've always wanted it to be. If you find you don't fit in the world, remake your part of it to fit to you. During this time, you will feel like you've figured out the secret of a happy life, and you may be correct, for now.

Ill-dignified: If surrounded by too many Swords and/or Air-based Major Arcana, this card can bring about wasted time, the wasting of money, and/or an utter lack of planning.

Prostitution by necessity is connected to this card. At worst, it brings about a total disconnect from the world around you.

Candy Darling (1944 – 1974) American trans actress and underground celebrity.

Candy was born a boy and spent her childhood in Long Island admiring and emulating the glamour of the great Hollywood stars, especially Kim Novak. However, she soon became Candy Darling and began frequenting Greenwich Village's trendiest night spots. In 1967, she met Andy Warhol (King of Coins) and appeared in several of his films, scene-stealing in *Flesh*, and starring in *Women in Revolt*, giving a comically rich and endearing performance.

After Warhol she went on to appear in mainstream movies with such notables as Jane Fonda (*Klute*) and Sophia Loren (*Lady Liberty*). She was cast in a staging of *Small Craft Warning* at Tennessee Williams's (The Moon) request.

Tragically, Candy died of lymphoma aged just twenty-nine. Her funeral was attended by thousands of well-wishers, among them the most famous names of the time – just as she would have wanted.

Candy Darling was her own special creation. She transformed herself, body and soul, to build a career and a legacy worthy of the Princess of Coins.

PRINCESS OF COINS

PRINCE OF COINS

This card's appearance in a reading heralds a time when determination, proficiency and practical energy assist you in getting a job done. You may also soon have a physical encounter or experience a financial situation from which steadfastness and thinking things through will be much-needed qualities, or you will meet someone of younger spirit, mind or age who will possess these attributes and be of great assistance. Now is the time when your competency, ingeniousness, and/or managerial skills will be put to the test, and they're sharper than they've ever been.

Ill-dignified: If surrounded by too many Swords and/or Air-based Major Arcana, this card is a warning against sloth, stoicism and tactlessness. You will feel stuck inside a routine of mundane actions, accomplishing nothing, and lacking the emotional responses to break free or understand the reactions of others.

Randy Shilts (1951 – 1994) Gay American journalist and writer at the center of documenting the AIDS epidemic and the struggle of LGBT people in the military.

In 1981, Randy Shilts became the first out journalist covering the gay community and specifically gay issues, just as gay men in major cities started dying of AIDS. Shilts would devote his life to documenting the epidemic and to exploring the social and political implications of the disease. His award-winning book *And the Band Played On: Politics, People, and the AIDS Epidemic*, remains the seminal account of the crisis. He also wrote *The Mayor of Castro Street*, a definitive biography of Harvey Milk (The Star*)* and addressed the issue of gays in the military in *Conduct Unbecoming*.

Although he was a leading gay voice of his time, he was criticized for his stance on closing bathhouses and his opposition to 'outing'. He died of AIDS in 1994.

It is Randy Shilts' practical energy and steadfast approach in bringing attention to the real issues of his day that make him the Prince of Coins. His writing challenged the establishment view of queers and ultimately helped redefine that view.

PRINCE OF COINS

QUEEN OF COINS

This card's appearance in a spread announces a time when you should consider solitude, calmness, and useful, practical work in your home environment. It is also a time for quiet ambition, to be useful and kind toward those around you who might be in financial or material need, or, you will meet someone of older heart, mind or age that is a provider to those less fortunate, a patron of the arts, or a generous parent figure who inspires through his or her example of living life to the fullest. They have lived a rich, storied, and fecund life thus far, have reached maturity beyond your own years, and can inform you about how best to create joy and security in your life. This card heralds bounty, domestication, the evocation of a life more charming, and the overall usefulness of giving one's time for another.

Ill-dignified: If surrounded by too many Swords or Air-based Major Arcana, this card is a warning against moodiness, an imbalance between work and family responsibilities, making capricious, foolish decisions, and an addiction to 'keeping up appearances'.

Ruth Ellis (1899 – 2000) Lesbian American activist who devoted her life to providing safe spaces for African American queers.

Born in Springfield, Illinois to a poor black family (her parents were born in the South during the last years of slavery), Ruth Ellis graduated high school when it was still rare for African Americans to do so. In spite of the social disadvantages she faced, Ruth came out as lesbian, formed an enduring relationship with Celine 'Babe' Franklin, and built her own business. Ruth later turned their home into a refuge and meeting place for black gays and lesbians. For decades, it was known as a safe place in Detroit.

In the 1970s, Ruth connected with other lesbian feminists and found herself and her experiences celebrated. Today, the Ruth Ellis Center offers support services to homeless and at-risk LGBT youth. Ruth herself attended the opening of the Center in 1999, just before her death.

Harnessing her generosity, compassion, and conscientiousness to change her environment and thereby the world, Ruth Ellis embodies the Queen of Coins. Her personal happiness was built on a stable domestic life and simply helping others.

QUEEN OF COINS

KING OF COINS

This card's appearance in a reading indicates a time when you can reap the rewards of a successful creative task, business endeavor, or investment. Through great discipline, solid instincts and material pragmatism you have accomplished much, and can now enjoy being the success that you are and have created. You have built a rich life, not just financially but also with regard to personal security and social standing. Your cleverness is perhaps singular, however, and you need to be careful not to become too preoccupied with maintaining the status quo, thereby missing out on aspects of life different from the ones you've focused on for so long. Regardless, this is a card of physical and material power and the acquisition of wealth and protections.

Ill-dignified: If surrounded by too many Swords or Air-based Major Arcana, this card heralds an utter lack of foresight, an incapability in finding an intelligent interest in anything outside of your own knowledge, and a jealousy of others' happiness when derived from non-materialistic means. It will also mean you'll spoil everything you touch.

Andy Warhol (1928 – 1987) Gay American artist, film director and producer; a leading figure of the Pop Art movement.

Born into a family of working-class Polish immigrants, Warhol trained as a commercial artist in Pittsburgh. Focusing on everyday objects (soup cans, cola bottles, dollar bills) or familiar images of celebrities (Marilyn Monroe, Elizabeth Taylor, Elvis Presley) repeated within the same frame/work, Warhol's pop art creations presented commentary on mass production, commercial branding, consumerism, and the nature of celebrity itself. His works, often produced by assistants, today sell for millions.

In the 1960s, he founded The Factory, a studio from which he produced art, made movies, and entertained many of the hippest media stars of the time. Warhol also co-produced and managed the seminal proto-punk band *The Velvet Underground*. He made dozens of experimental movies and created a stable of Warhol starlets, including Candy Darling (Princess of Coins). In 1968, he was shot and seriously injured by Valerie Solanas (Princess of Swords).

Andy Warhol reaped the rewards of his creative success. Like the King of Coins, he built material security and acquired social status. Ironically, Warhol's paintings, once a critique, are now the ultimate status symbol and a solid business investment.

KING OF COINS

MODERN QUEER TAROT
MERCHANDISE